Paint Effects

Paint Effects

a practical guide

Johan de Villiers • Len Straw

HUMAN & ROUSSEAU
Cape Town   Pretoria   Johannesburg

We would like to thank
PLASCON
whose generous sponsorship made
publication of this book possible.

This book is dedicated with gratitude to
Anne van Zyl.

Copyright © 1996 by Johan de Villiers and Len Straw
First published in 1996 by Human & Rousseau (Pty) Ltd
State House, 3-9 Rose Street, Cape Town
Photography by Juan Espi and Len Straw
Typography and cover design by Etienne van Duyker
Text electronically prepared in 10 on 14 pt Ultima Light
Colour reproduction by CMYK, Cape Town
Printed and bound by Colorcraft, Hong Kong

0 7981 3548 4

Contents

Sponsor's foreword

*I*n 1986, Plascon became seriously involved for the first time with paint techniques. We were not sure if it would be a passing "fad" but nevertheless in 1989, the first Plascon Paint Techniques book was published. To our surprise and delight, paint techniques proved far more successful than had been envisaged and futher reprints were required.

As decorating has proved to be such a rewarding pastime and profession, paint techniques in South Africa has become well established and has developed into a mini-industry in the process.

With the growth in application, new techniques have evolved, old techniques have been refined and developed, and so the need has arisen for a new book on the subject. We are proud to be associated with well-known decorative artists Len Straw and Johan de Villiers in the production of this book on the art of paint techniques.

Both Len and Johan have extensive experience with decorative paint techniques and have been involved in many prestigious projects such as The Bay Hotel in Cape Town.

After two years of exacting work, Len and Johan have succeeded in capturing all the creative potential of decorating with paint on these pages. We believe their showcase will empower you to achieve your creative potential too!

Enjoy it!

Peter Surgey
Group Managing Director, Plascon

Foreword

I first met Len and Johan in 1982 while they were lecturing and demonstrating paint techniques at an interior decorating seminar at Josephine Mill in Cape Town. It was my first introduction to the various paint techniques and I was fascinated. That was the start of our happy association which has resulted in our working together ever since, organising courses, editorials and interior decorating shows for my retail customers.

At the time Len was doing commissioned decorative painting, while Johan was a successful art teacher at the Frank Joubert Art Centre. As all decorative painters know only too well, building up contacts and becoming known in this competitive industry is an extremely difficult process. I was privileged to see their business grow until, in 1990, Johan took the bold step of leaving the teaching profession and joining Len as a full-time decorative painter. They opened their studio in 1st Avenue, Claremont at about the same time and began operating under the name of Paint Effects. I remember Len saying that they appeared to be much busier but not much richer – but I am sure that has now changed! As Paint Effects they have an impressive list of painting achievements, including the Lanzerac Manor House, Constantia Uitsig, the Peninsula Hotel, many domestic interiors and even a guest house in Greece and a project in Paris.

Paint techniques are not normally tackled for their own sake. They form part of an overall decorating plan or project requiring subtlety of both colour and technique. Len and Johan successfully manage to convey this and other decorating aspects in their teaching. Working as a team, providing humour and alternating regularly between English and Afrikaans to meet the requirements of their audience, they pass on those practical tips that their years of experience have taught them. Experience and talent are also needed to work as fast and as neatly as they do – I never tire of watching Johan marbling at speed while speaking into a microphone at the same time. Many interior decorators, architects, specialist painters and DIY enthusiasts have benefited from their artistry and the communication skills they have used over the years to pass on their love of decorating. I hope they never stop teaching – the industry needs them. At present *Garden & Home* magazine and Plascon Paints make extensive use of their expertise in this field.

I regard this book as an extension of teaching and communicating the enjoyment derived from decorative painting – the only difference being that it is aimed at a wider audience.

Len Straw and Johan de Villiers travel overseas regularly to undertake commissions, to participate in highly specialised courses and to absorb the cultures and colours of other countries, thus broadening their understanding of this vast subject. They are always bristling with new ideas and I am pleased that they now have the opportunity to share some of them with you. May this book inspire you to new creative heights!

Norman Armstrong

Introduction

The art of decorative painting is not easy to define or compartmentalise. On the one hand it links up with the work of plasterers and painters and on the other hand it could become fine art. Even at the time of Leonardo da Vinci and Michelangelo decorated interiors evoked great interest and provided endless joy.

Sadly, the general impression of paint effects today is that of walls being vigorously and carelessly rubbed, sponged and spattered by undisciplined people wearing tired clothing!

The truth of the matter is that good results can only be procured if the artist knows his tools and media, listens to his client and works discreetly towards a neat and technically sound end result. An ultimate gauge of success invariably is the joyful satisfaction of both client and artist. We are frequently surprised at the way in which beautifully and appropriately coloured textured walls pull a scheme together.

Flat colour refers to regular painting. Broken colour, on the other hand, refers to undulating tones, pattern, texture and changing colour. Various degrees are possible: soft off-white, sandy tones to brilliantly saturated primaries or rich deep antique reds.

Strictly speaking, paint techniques can be divided into glazing, graining and marbling. Each of these has its ground rules as well as, in the hands of an accomplished artist, its derivatives. The serious reader will soon understand that this book attempts to inspire visually. This leads to enquiry and subsequently to discovery and practice. In other words: see the picture, flip the page, read and do!

Beautiful things have always formed an important part of our lives. Inspired by antiquity, just old things, yesterday's things, today and tomorrow's things, we collect, glean ideas and put together various pieces. Some people call it decorating! Thus, 20 years ago, it happened that we became particularly enchanted with the never-ending possibilities offered by the painted surface. Initially we absorbed facts, inspiration and technical skills by reading overseas magazines and books. The need for practical experience prompted us to paint our own home and furniture.

We opened a restaurant which we decorated – our first venture into the public eye. This was soon followed by a sponged interior for the Cape Town couturier Errol Arendz's new salon. We were launched!

All this preamble serves only to encourage our readers – with one very important reservation: no success can be expected without hard physical and mental work.

A prime reason for producing this book is to encourage South Africans to use local products and designs freely and without hesi-

tation. We used to guess what the various overseas products were – with greater or lesser success. This is not the ideal method; consequently we provide a list of products and their local names or substitutes (see page 141) on which our methods are based. We have even provided exact recipes in some cases. These basics, sensibly used, will provide an invaluable foundation.

Learning through experience can be exhilarating, challenging and tremendously exciting, but uncertainty and doubt frequently render one helpless, inhibiting production. As soon as we felt ready for specialist tuition, we enrolled for two courses in England. Our first teacher was a professional decorator who had started at the bottom as a young boy and acquired his skills through hard work and tenacity. We experienced a little of the life of a journeyman – with exactly the results we were aiming for. From early in the morning until late afternoon we learnt, did and redid; picking up many of the tricks of the trade that no publication can ever provide. Bless Tim Dudfield of Newent, Gloucestershire.

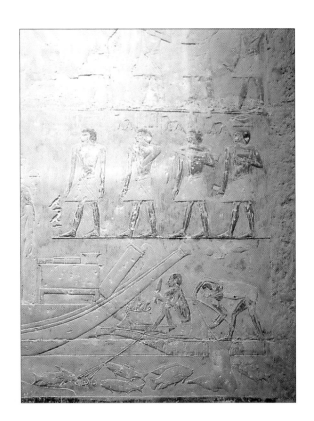

Completely different but equally generous with his information was Roger Newton of the London School of Decorative Painting. He ran a school in London and provided a restoration service to various dealers and renowned auctioneers. Observing in his busy studio we learnt a great deal about gilding and antiquing. He handled period work and current trends with equal facility and aplomb.

Fortuitously these teachers covered all the aspects of a complex trade − notably a thorough basic working knowledge of media, tools, colour and design as well as awareness of and sensitivity to current movements, fashion and demand.

We endeavour to show in this book how we glean inspiration from everything around us: lichen on an old oak tree, the patina of old worn leather, spring-green leaves pushing up through bright orange soil, Van Gogh's tormented skies or the sumptuous marble of the palace of Versailles. Look and see: every day will provide countless revelations for your delight.

In view of this, how can people say that decorative painting is a fad, a passing fancy that will wither and die like a seasonal flower? Man has been decorating his abode since time immemorial. We still marvel at paintings in caves and on rocks all over the world. Etruscan, Cretan and Egyptian paintings and friezes render us spellbound. Much of what we know about the history of various civilizations was revealed to us through the remains of their arts.

In fact, the very period of austerity and lack of decoration that causes one to doubt continuity of paint effects was a very deliberate effort against such ornamentation, the point being that the human inclination is towards adornment and that the elimination of such can only be achieved through positive effort. The beauty and unsurpassed quality of many of the Bauhaus products can only be ascribed to hard work.

The world has been happily rag-rolling, dragging, sponging and stippling for approximately fifteen years now. These techniques have become popular and general. Artists have developed the basics, adapting and

extending towards more exciting and sophisticated finishes. Selected surfaces are treated to contrast with their environment, with subtlety becoming the password. Thoughtless painting of every conceivable surface is definitely not appropriate these days.

Far from having become tedious and unexciting, the stage of five-finger exercises is over and we are now aspiring towards imaginative concertos! At times it is still necessary to imitate nature, reproducing perfect woodgrain or marble, but the age of fantasy finishes has dawned. Instead of imitative copying of nature, a new spirit of imagination is resulting in an enthusiastic move towards abstraction. Instead of using small swirls of green malachite on a modest box, the effects can now cover an entire wall with bold colour and pattern; only a suggestion of nature remains, the rest is pure invention.

Another expensive paint finish which is currently in demand, requires great skill and paradoxically looks like aged and neglected surfaces. Cracks are painted across faded, weather-beaten walls. Wood is given a cracked and chipped finish while moulded forms have recesses with dark "gunge" highlighting their contours. Presumably escapist, these techniques allow us to create patinated red leathery panels associated with an English library, or painterly dusty terracotta Florentine walls or even sunbaked cracked adobe desert surfaces.

Readers who contemplate chipping away their textured, stippled, plastered walls, are advised that the three-dimensional finishes are coming back! Sometimes glazes or paints are applied to textured surfaces while the ultimate finish now requires a build-up of layers of pigmented plasters. This is a sophisticated finish and beyond the scope of the dilettante.

Our contention is that there is a great future for paint effects. Admittedly some aspects have been overexposed, but so much remains to be explored, developed and enjoyed that the painted surface cannot but amuse us for many years to come!

Colour

*O*ur aim is not to discuss the *science* as much as the *joy* of glorious colour. Watching a group of little children – all new art students – discover colour is a precious moment. If they are limited to the primary colours – blue, red and yellow – they initially use them as they are. Soon, however, they discover mixing and with some luck they will produce the secondary colours green, orange and purple – and a great variety of hideous mud! Give them white as well and they may produce colours that look like strawberry ice cream, sky blue or vanilla pudding.

Primaries or secondaries with white added are referred to as tints. Colours with black added are referred to as shades. Through a few basic exercises these little students will develop the ability to manipulate their colours. We use the analogy of children in order to explain the natural development of skills and therefore the universal pattern for all of us.

The same fascination with colour remains with us throughout our lives. When we teach our basic paint techniques courses we again provide the students with paint in primary colours and white. Some of these students have not had any previous painting or colour-mixing experience. Initially they are filled with fear and trepidation but soon one hears shrieks of delight: "That's just the turquoise I want!" Our aim is to encourage students to get involved in order to be able to decide how to adjust colours to their needs.

Colour is arbitrary. Everyone experiences colour in a very personal way. The same colour seen in daylight changes dramatically at night. One colour painted throughout a room could appear markedly different on the various walls depending on the light. The colour chips from the Plascon Computacolor range are a great help to the painter as long as he realises that larger areas of these same colours can look startlingly different.

On the odd occasion a client has a specific colour in mind. This is rather awkward since an isolated colour "in one's mind" is difficult to mix and will certainly change on a wall, in sunlight, in lamplight or in a shaded area. Eventually you should be delighted by the various nuances of your chosen colour rather than exhaust yourself trying to get an exact, constant hue. After all, this is the magic of colour!

Some people select colours in a totally spontaneous way. They like a colour and that is it. Such decisions are mostly good because they reflect a certain character and any additional decorating would show the same quality and mood. Similarly, rapid decisions can be made by designers, artists and painters who have a solid colour background. Familiarity with the effects and interactions of colours allows spontaneous selection which never ceases to amaze one. However, the most popular and best way to choose colours is to draw colour swatches, to apply colour samples, to contemplate, to change – in fact, to work hard at it!

The little art students at the Frank Joubert Art Centre develop a facility for analysing paintings at a very early age. Sitting on the floor in the museum the little eyes dart across a modern painting no adult seems to understand. With some guidance they pick out the bright colours, the dominant colours, the light ones, dark ones and the dull ones. Soon they realise that certain colours form strong contrasts while others harmonise gently. A small spot of bright colour might jump out at you while its dull background recedes magically. These concepts are basic and very important, they are easy to identify and to understand, yet they are extremely difficult to implement. The little ones initially create their colour focal points with disastrous ineptitude but as time passes, working at it, they produce more and more coherent work. Our type of painting demands hard work and an experimental spirit. Only after many years of colour work do we now with great circumspection choose colours for an area.

Referring to the work involved, it could help the reader if we explain how we go about using colour. Initially we get to know the clients and their aims. This also includes wandering into other areas of their homes to gauge their taste, boldness, likes and dislikes, etc. An analysis of the area in question would require a study of furnishings, textiles, flooring, lighting (natural and artificial), and dimensions. Slowly various options emerge. Drawing from our colour charts and sample boards we eventually decide on both colour and technique. Large sample boards are prepared in the actual colours and techniques.

These are left with the client to peruse at leisure over a weekend or longer. We advise them to move the boards around the rooms and to consider the appearance at night. It is not unusual for a client to request a sample on the wall. In this case it is advisable to use an area neatly framed by a door and window frame or to demarcate an area. Splashes of colour and tattily daubed techniques do not enhance either the trade or one's reputation. In both your and the clients' interest it is advisable to ask them to sign the appropriate sample boards on acceptance.

With repetitive mixing, we urge painters to have colours mixed to colour-chart specifications rather than to trust their aptitude and memory. The greatest of colour mixers get it wrong before they get it right!

If you are confronted by blank walls, blank stares from clients and a request for a total colour scheme, you have to find inspiration from *any* source – no matter how many colour variations you have used in the past. Nature, for instance, shows us multitudes of different hues, combinations and contrasts. To this end we have collected and compiled a great number of photographs of various subjects. The exercise has helped us considerably to become even more aware – to look, but also to see. This very point was aptly illustrated by a new young pupil who arrived at his classes in a state of euphoria. His friends, he discovered, could not see what he saw. The bark of trees was not just brown or grey; they were real colours. And his companions did not even notice the bark!

The same lack of perception was also evident when a visitor looked at our subtly sponged sitting-room walls some years ago, frowned and asked what the matter was with them!

Once an awareness of colour and texture has been developed, your creativity comes to the fore and soon marvellous things present themselves. There is absolutely no excuse for a lack of ideas. The world around us is filled with colour, ingenious harmonies and astounding contrasts.

In decoration the harmonious use of colours or tones depends on their closeness to one another. Referring to a colour wheel or a rainbow, colours occurring alongside one another are harmonious, for example blue, turquoise and green, or yellow, orange and red. These combinations are straightforward and need not be daunting. They are beautiful and can stand on their own.

Much more challenging, exciting and obviously frightening is the use of contrasts. These can be tonal (light and dark) or colour contrasts. The strongest tonal contrast is illustrated by black and white, while blue/orange, yellow/purple and red/green are obvious and really powerful colour contrasts. An analogy here would be the "old-fashioned" use of beige: seeing it as a safe colour, feeling at home in neither the stark white nor the brightly hued interiors of the sixties and the seventies, the home decorator of the time opted for gentle, similar and unadventurous shades of beige. Neutral beige was the pass-word and contrasts were all but ignored.

Beige is back today, but in many guises … dark, light, grey, brown and cream. They are contrasted with each other, and with black, charcoal, white, rust and other colours. Even the rich tones of natural wood are used as foils. This gives rise to bold, free-spirited deco-rating which has the edge on conservative work.

It is gratifying to know, however, that colour or shade contrasts do not have to be strong. Subtle differences can create excel-lent effects provided another aspect, such as texture, is introduced. The natural hues of stone, hessian, bark, gravel, wood, etc. would, as flat colours, present a rather monotonous palette. As soon as their textures are brought into account, a different picture emerges. This often accounts for the use of broken-colour techniques or textural finishes on walls.

Every now and then we witness an acci-dental contrast or plain mismatching which in fact proves to be an absolute delight. A lime-green knee rug was accidentally left in a calico-and-other-naturals-only sitting room. It now lives there permanently with several other

similarly hued objects! In another instance the only washed and ironed cushion covers in the linen drawer were in bright cerise … placed on the bedcover, a ruddy khelim, they lifted an aspect from its various colours that astounded us. Now there is a replacement pair of cerise covers! Being too bold with these rather strange contrasts, however, we are all too often put in our place when our contrived "accidental" schemes look it!

While it is possible to write at length about colour and its many fascinating theories and qualities, we would just like to touch on a few very basic aspects as they impact on the decorative painter.

Choosing colour from a small chip can be hazardous. Large areas of exactly the same colour can be frighteningly strong or quite ineffective. Once a colour has been selected, it is imperative to try it out. This colour could be a standard off-the-shelf hue or mixed according to colour samples from the Plascon Computacolor range or from the International Colour Chart. Bear in mind that your own recipe for "that magical colour" would be extremely difficult to repeat in a paint-shop situation.

There is no exception – colours change character depending on light and shade. Paint neat patches of colour in various parts of the room and consider them at different times of the day. Tattily slapped on paint splodges will neither appear good nor enhance your respect for your own work. Do not be tempted simply to fiddle with a pre-mixed colour. Ask your paint dealer to adjust it with measured amounts of pigment. Take note of the exact quantities of these additions with a view to repeating the mixture. Should you be forced to do the adjusting yourself it is advisable to use measuring spoons or cups. Write down how you achieve the colours. You seldom remember the exact amounts you have been adding, little by little, by the time you eventually arrive at the desired colour! Various pigments can be used to modify colours. Mixing in paler or stronger hues of the same type of paint is the very simplest method. Oil-based paints are only compatible with other oil-based products.

Universal stainers are strong pigments suitable for adding to either water- or oil-based paints. They are available in little tubes or bottles. It is advisable to mix some stainer into a small quantity of the paint before adding it little by little to the big tin of paint. In the case

of water-based paints you can add some water to facilitate a smooth mixture and in the case of oils you would use some turpentine.

Aim towards finishing a full wall before changing to a new tin of paint – especially if you have done your own mixing. Subtle differences can occur and changing in a corner will obviate any problems.

Another option is powdered pigments like the so-called school paint or powdered tempera. Again you need to mix them with either water (plus a drop of dishwashing liquid) or turpentine before adding them to the pots of water-based or oil-based paints respectively.

An interesting recent development is the return to natural pigments and natural media. A most successful and beautiful finish on the exterior walls of a Johannesburg home with a North African appearance was attained by using ordinary red ochre soil and red iron oxide as pigments and slaked lime and a bonding liquid as media. The result was a glowing earthy colour similar to the mud houses of the indigenous people of North Africa. It also made the painter a very happy man when the realisation dawned that he was in fact doing almost what his mother used to do to their kaya years ago!

Unfortunately we do not have a recipe for this technique and can only advise experimentation.

With the "new" natural pigments go natural media: water, buttermilk, vinegar, egg yolk, sugar and other very ordinary commodities. Thus we still use traditional methods for both vinegar painting and woodgraining. It is a joy to read in Cennini's *Il libro dell'arte* how one gets a certain black by incinerating vine twigs and grinding them to powder. The most perfect black is made from almond shells or peach stones! Thank goodness for the apprentices who did all the hard work in those days.

But back to colour as such. Using broken-colour techniques and glazes often leaves one surprised (pleasantly or otherwise), helpless or amazed! Results are very seldom totally predictable and adjustments are the rule rather than the exception. Since these colour adjustments are done in specific ways for each technique, they will be explained as the techniques are described. For the time being we want to assure the reader that we never paint out – we would much rather work over and over disappointments. They are the ones that turn into the best rooms ever!

Blue

It is no good fighting a brick wall! Taking advantage of the texture, the walls of this bedroom have been glazed in shades and tints of blues. Anchoring the wall is a broad skirting streaked in dark blue. The sleigh bed and occasional table have been painted and streaked in a softer blue. A powdery terracotta floor provides lightness to complement the softly draped mosquito net.

We used to see bagged brick walls as an obstacle, wondering what we could do to change them. When an architect called us in to do something to a single brick wall in an otherwise plastered room, it dawned on us that this wall was special in this context and we realised that we could use its texture instead of fighting it. Two glazes of almost alarming red hues transformed the wall into a most effective talking point.

The brick wall in our illustration was painted with white Plascon Polvin as a base. A Tallangatta Blue Polvin (T83-4) and Plascon Water-based Glazecoat mixture of equal parts was made and painted on with a 100 mm paintbrush. The method reflects "clouding" where one loads the brush with glaze (or paint) and paints an area, fading out the edges. So one continues butting one area up against another, starting a new cloud or leaving areas of white. The glaze dries very quickly and one can deepen colours by overlaying glazes, but take care only to work on perfectly dry surfaces. This is how we attained the deep blue around the perimeter of the wall. The almost white area on the other hand has only the slightest of glaze wash over it.

With the application of a glaze the brick texture inevitably becomes more pronounced and in addition to colour the glaze also provides a soft sheen. Such a finish gives a brick wall a new status.

Accessories

Our sleigh bed has been washed in slightly diluted Polvin, Iron Grey (M32-8). A coat of wax polish provides a soft sheen and has provided ample protection over the past five years.

The bedside table had a varnished finish which was duly sanded down to provide a key for a coat of Plascon Glazecoat (CV82) tinted with Blue Knight Velvaglo (45-17M). The reason we used Oil-based Glazecoat was to prevent our blue from turning green the way that regular polyurethane varnish would. After one coat of tinted varnish, we sanded some of it away for a distressed look. Two protective coats of CV82 Oil-based Glazecoat followed. Then a light sanding with very fine waterpaper, and finally we polished it with wax polish.

3. The grooved boards below the dado rail were painted a flat Blue Tulle, Plascon Polvin, while the dado rail and skirting board were painted Creole, Plascon Polvin. We chose to use Polvin on the woodwork in order to obtain a soft powdery look. One could seal everything with Glazecoat Clear Matt, but it would kill the look with its inevitable ever-so-slight sheen.

Accessories

The simple wooden table (page 28) is one of a pair that we found. They used to be small wash stands but lost their lovely decorative towel rails and acquired many coats of paint before we stripped them again. We did not clean out the residue paint from their nooks and crannies and grain. The whiteness now gives them the appearance of having been limewashed. Rickety but pretty, it is laden with interesting flotsam and jetsam from the beach.

Above the dado rail we pasted on moulded resin shells, each rubbed with Polvin which was then rubbed off in parts. More resin shells were stuck to an ordinary wooden frame which was treated similarly with blue Polvin rubbed on and off.

An old key box from an office encases a natural terracotta starfish set against a blue background. The little glazed box was "limewashed" with diluted white Polvin.

The sturdy kitchen chairs upholstered in thick calico were stained dark before they were crackled in grey-blue, Iron Grey Polvin (M32-8). See page 111 for the craquelure technique.

Blue / green

*This blue-green scene conjures up a country atmosphere in a refreshingly neat way.
The timber wall, initially white, has been streaked in both green and blue with
ample white shining through. Against this crisp background we set an old stripped
meat-safe with its green pigmentation still clearly in evidence. A dark-green-stained
wicker chair, a glass fishing float and an Indian hundi lamp contrast strongly.
Temptation to reframe the two 1940s watercolours was overcome in favour of
historical and artistic correctness!*

A white tongue-and-groove board wall in knotty pine can quite easily be depressingly dull. The warmth of the wood is not always conducive to the crisp look of a beach cottage. There is often very little to redeem a very "knotty" ceiling and painting it is no crime. Some boards have knots that never seem to stop oozing resin. Treat such problem knots with Plascon's Woodcore Knotting (PK2), a spirit-based sealer.

Our wall had been painted with white Polvin before we started on this project. Bear in mind that a previously varnished wall will need to be sanded down to provide a key or "grip". Subsequently a coat of Plascon Merit Universal Undercoat should be rolled or brushed on. Although oil-based, the surface will be matt and will take a coat of Plascon White Polvin (PVA) quite readily.

While a single colour would have been effective, we chose to use two colours: Plascon's Mod Blue and Mod Green, both in Polvin. Dish a few tablespoonfuls of each colour into an enamel plate or a paint tray. Keep a shallow dish of water handy. Using an emulsion or similar brush, pick up some of the green paint sparingly. Streak this onto the boards working fast and along the length of the board. Should the full-strength Polvin be too thick and unresponsive, moisten the tips of the bristles in water and continue the streaking. Change colour from time to time but be sure to rid the brush of one colour before you pick up the next. Always work with a "dry" brush, allowing lots of the white base to show through.

Initially it is difficult to maintain a balance between the colours as well as between a wet and dry brush. Do not give up! And remember that an overcoloured area can quite easily be streaked over in the white Polvin base colour. It is not necessary to seal the wall but if you really have to, Plascon Glazecoat Clear Matt (REF. 1125) will be the appropriate product.

Accessories

The old meat-safe (page 32) is one of those pieces that one does not see too often these days. Instead of stripping the paint off to bare wood, we left some green and white pigment but smoothened all surfaces with fine sandpaper. We decided against a coat of varnish but used Cobra White Floor Wax to lend it a used and nicely worn patina.

To stain wicker is quite easy, provided it is raw and unvarnished. Stains such as Plascon Woodstain are easily available in wood colours such as Oak, Imbuia, etc. For brighter colours you have to use aniline dyes. They are used by leather workers and we know how colourfast leather goods are. These dyes are very concentrated and we usually dilute them with methylated spirits. Wear gloves and a mask for protection when working with these. One can brush the dyes on but spraying is easier and it reaches into nooks and crannies. The dye penetrates the surface, does not rub off and remains colourfast.

A coat or two of polyurethane varnish will provide an excellent finished surface. This way you create a depth of colour even more glowing and translucent than a scumble glaze.

It is not easy for a painter to resist repainting such things as the hat boxes and picture frames. However, it is exactly the strange, worn-away, old painted surfaces of the boxes that imbue them with a special character. So, we simply washed them well and there were our occasional tables . . . ready to use! The picture frames were a much easier decision: framing can be expensive and these perfectly good frames were the originals. We think that keeping them like that would have pleased the artists and in addition the wood and black colours suited the setting perfectly!

Green

Brilliant colours are set against a blue-green sponged background. Skirtings are in yellow-green. The textural theme is extended to the leopard-spotted cupboard frame. A simple dark Tallangatta Blue in Polvin (T83-4) lines the inside of the cupboard and is also the colour used on the kitchen chair. Bright touches are provided by ceramics and innovatively designed linen cushions.

Green: Step by step

RAG-ROLLING ON

This technique is quite easy – even for the novice! It can be a rather messy process, though, and if not carefully executed, it can look it too!

1. Initially, roll or paint on a fine coat of a chosen base colour in Polvin (PVA) or any other water-based product. In this case we used Dillweed Green (M38-4 Plascon Computacolor).

2. Subsequently a water-based glaze should be mixed up, using two parts Plascon Water-based Glazecoat (REF. 1125) to one part Polvin. Our choice of colour to complement our base coat was Henty Green (U81-3 Plascon Computacolor). If you would rather not use a glaze which gives a slight translucency, it would also be in order to use a somewhat diluted Polvin (three parts paint to one part water).

3. Pour some of this second colour into a paint tray or a flat enamel dish. Get three or four pieces of cotton or other firm cloth ready. They must be similar in texture and size. At this stage we put on our gloves – the mess is about to start!

4. Roll one of the pieces of cloth into a *loose* sausage shape. Pick up some paint from the tray by rolling the piece of cloth through the puddle. Roll it with very little pressure along the flat part of the tray. Should you be working from a dish, roll onto a piece of hardboard, cardboard or wherever you can ensure that the paint gets evenly distributed along your rolled-up cloth.

5. Having removed the excess paint, the actual rolling can proceed. Work at an angle of approximately 45 degrees. Roll lightly and resist the temptation to squeeze the rag out against the wall. This is a sure way of creating blotches. Should such blemishes occur, they must be left to dry before you roll over them again in the base colour. Breaking them up again is the magic solution. Take care not to overload the rag but, similarly, do not work with too dry a cloth. Open the cloth up from time to time to change the imprint. Remember to keep your cloth loosely rolled, not too tight. It is also good to change direction and to fill in bald spots, using the rag scrunched into a loose rose shape in the palm of your hand instead of twisting it into a cylinder. This would also be the way to get into the most awkward areas. Do not over-work corners and edges along cornices and skirting boards. An underworked halo along the perimeter of a wall is much better than an overworked, messy edge.

6. Paint skirting boards last of all (we used a Mod Green Polvin which appears quite lime against the blue-green walls). They always provide a neat finish. Touch up cornices for the same reason.

Regarding the choice of colours, strong hues and contrasts create the textural quality we show in our main picture. The variety of bright colours prompted us in this direction. For a subtle version a marginally darker base with a lighter rag-rolling over it would be ideal. Various colours rag-rolled over one another could be most successful, but must be tested on a piece of sample board beforehand.

Accessories

Our cupboard (page 36) used to be a small wardrobe, now fitted with shelves to accommodate linen. This rather sad-looking cupboard was stripped before it was painted in white Plascon Polvin. The whole exterior was then rubbed in a water-based glaze of Manor Cream (M34-1 Plascon Computacolor). While the panels were left as they were, the framework has been rubbed here and there in Polvin Ascot Tan glaze. Over these brownish surfaces we then stencilled leopard spots! The blue inside is alas not an original idea.

We saw a beautiful old wardrobe at an antique market in Provence (above). The outside was weathered and well used, with lots of character and history … and the inside was a bright blue. Once we had completed our cupboard it was sealed with Glazecoat. The blue kitchen chair received the same treatment.

The blue plates on the wall (page 36) are loosely based on the design of some plates we purchased in the South of France some years ago. A local manufacturer produced them exclusively for us for a year … now they are freely available as their "French" plates!

Ochre

A stylish but welcoming sitting room in a Franschhoek farmhouse. The rural quality of this setting required an informal paint finish and the walls were therefore sponged and glazed. Colour combinations are relaxed and accessories range from treasured French ceramics to the children's collection of guinea-fowl feathers in a wire basket.

*O*chre can prove to be a very troublesome colour. We know it is a sunny, joyful, warm hue, but we have also experienced the feeling of being in a bowl of egg yolk when we were actually aiming at a gentle primula colour! Of the ochre interiors we have seen, the most remarkable was a London drawing room painted in ochre touched with green. The silken drapes, swags and curtains were of a similar hue. Within this ochre cocoon was a collection of English antiques, superb modern and period paintings in antique gold frames and upholstery and rugs in gentle terracottas, spring-leaf green and dusty blue. Somehow we have never been able to use this scheme in South Africa. Could it have something to do with the English light …?

Quite different − but no less delightful − was our choice of French Mustard in Polvin (D34-8) for the Franschhoek farmhouse sitting room. Admittedly it was a contrived choice: we had just returned from Provence, our clients are decided Francophiles and the Franschhoek light, style and general ambience demanded *mustard*.

Ochre: Step by step

1. We requested the walls to be painted pure white (Plascon Polvin White) to start with. Our first step was to sponge the walls in an undiluted Plascon Polvin (French Mustard) using a natural sea sponge. Always moisten your marine sponge with water and squeeze it dry before you use it. Spoon a small amount of the French Mustard Polvin into an enamel plate or any shallow dish. Pick up some of this paint with the sponge by gently touching the surface of the paint puddle. Do not over-

load the sponge and, using a sheet of plain white newsprint or some roller towel, test your sponge imprint before blotching the wall! Bear in mind that a sponge is a soft and gentle tool. Treat it accordingly by applying little pressure – just enough to create a clear imprint. Sponge random patterns over the wall, aiming at a spontaneous distribution of densely and sparsely textured areas. Standing back at this stage can prove very disturbing since the walls will now appear to be suffering from an acute attack of mustard measles! To keep your mind otherwise occupied, you could treat the areas where you have made ugly blotches by simply sponging over them in your base colour – in this case white.

2. Now you can mix a water-based glaze using one part of Plascon Water-based Glazecoat (Matt) and half a part of French Mustard Polvin. Use either a cheap commer-cial sponge or a piece of cloth to pick up a small amount of glaze. We also sometimes apply the glaze to the sponge or piece of cloth with a paintbrush. This way you avoid picking up too much glaze. Rub it onto the wall as if you are washing it. Waste no time to rub out the edges, i.e. they must fade out to nothing-ness. Do not rub square patches; it is better to work randomly and bear in mind that this is a broken-colour technique which implies that there will be darker and lighter areas. Use a brush to finish off the corners, the skirting and the cornices as neatly as possible. The strong contrast of white wall and mustard sponging will have been softened by now.

3. Unfortunately the job is not over yet! In order to refine the patina a second rubbing is absolutely essential. The effort put into this final coat unfailingly cures the tired arm and dispels whatever misgivings there may have been regarding your competence.

Red

This rich red leathery look appeals to most people — and it is used too seldom. Various ruddy tones, dark wood, gilt and the sumptuous colour and texture of the carpet create an elegant setting. Hand-painted panels on the walls were done in pale yellow but appear gold when rubbed with an antiquing glaze.

Red: Step by step

Our method refers to a red wall but the same procedure can be followed to create this technique in any other colour. Bear in mind that it works better in some colours than in others, but taste has much to do with it.

Instead of a white surface a red base is called for. An excellent colour is Plascon Polvin Mod Red which is, like all the other Mod Polvins, the purest and most saturated primary or secondary colour available off the shelf. It is to your advantage to roll the red on randomly. This will result in an overall mottled appearance. A second coat will not be necessary unless the colour being painted out underneath is violent and persistent. As is often the case with initial painting, the appearance of walls at this stage can be rather offensive. Subsequently you must mix a glaze to create an antique patina over the red. Quantities are not very specific and can be adjusted darker or lighter to suit your needs. Our medium for this glaze, however, is Plascon Water-based Glazecoat, Clear Matt. Stir it well before you use it. Use one cup of Glazecoat to half a cup of Mod Red (or whatever colour you are working with) and add modest but measured amounts of Buffalo Universal Stainer in Brown. Mix these ingredients very well before testing in an obscure spot. This mixture dries very quickly and must be wiped away as soon as you have seen the quality. The aim is to patinate the harsh red with a darker shade. Since the mixture is translucent and only the pigments are opaque, the resultant effect has an intriguingly *chiaroscuro* vitality. Work with a manageable − small − quantity of glaze on your synthetic sponge and rub out the edges (see ochre rubbing, page 43). A second rubbing will produce a darker but infinitely improved result.

 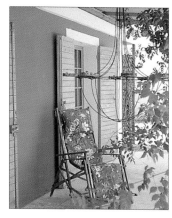 

Terracotta

A soft cloudy or nebulous effect provides a graceful background to a very distressed table, a small stencilled and crackled cupboard and a stencil-motif fabric which we have called Carol's Harvest. The variegated ficus continues the "green" and "leaf" themes.

A… ahem … retired woman friend of ours told us recently how they, as young salesladies at Harrods, were taught to refer to the colours of outfits in a way that would be most attractive to prospective female customers. Chartreuse, Burgundy, Taupe, Aubergine rather than pale green, maroon, donkey and eggplant! Names are supposed to be positively descriptive but sometimes there is so much leeway that utter confusion ensues. In the search for a fine terracotta which should be a no-mistake earth red, one could land up with anything from cool peach to burnt orange, from rust to brick or coral to gravel. Clients who have a colour in mind are often surprised at our interpretation of their terracotta. We have come to accept many a terracotta as the correct one! It would be silly to jeopardise a perfectly good relationship for the sake of a few drops of brown universal tinter! Which brings us to the crux of the matter, we think: the necessity of a browny tinge to terracotta. In our classes we encourage students to experiment with mixing a terracotta. They start with a rather alarming mixture of red and yellow to result in an orange. A touch of blue turns it into a brown mixture. Depending on the quantities of the three ingredients, you may get a red, yellow or brown terracotta. To arrive at a soft powdery colour you simply add some of this concentrated mixture to white until you get what you need.

Some of our most successful terracottas have been:
● Rock Melon (Plascon M52-4), a browny pink-orange, a strong colour;
● Melon Glow (Plascon M52-2), an orangey-pink, also strong;
● Smoked Salmon (Plascon M52-3), browny-orange;
● Candlelight (Plascon P22-4), bronzey but soft;
● Blushing Rose (Plascon M21-5), decidedly pink;
● Terracotta – Plascon Wall and All.

The wall illustrated on the previous page was done in a technique called clouding which is straightforward and uncomplicated. Select a terracotta or use the one we did: Antique Coral (International 12-18D) in Plascon Polvin. You will also need a tin of White Plascon Polvin, an emulsion or similar brush (100 mm) and a smaller paintbrush (50 mm), a few plastic or old kitchen spoons and a large plain enamel plate. Scoop a few spoonfuls of white Polvin and a lesser quantity of Antique Coral into the plate. It does not matter if they blend a bit.

Pick up some white Polvin with the emulsion brush and apply it to the wall, painting an irregular area and feathering out the edges. Carry on painting until the brush is really dry. Only then do you pick up some of the Antique Coral which should not be painted over the white but as an extension to it. As soon as the brush is free of paint, you can return to the area between the white and Antique Coral to blend them into each other. Should the blending prove to be awkward because the paint dries too quickly, you could moisten the tips of the bristles slightly with some water every now and then. The process is repeated with soft "clouds" of colour being formed in a sea of white. The size, shape and intensity of the "clouds" will depend on your taste and requirements. We tend to move across a wall at a slight angle, lending some movement to the effect. Provided you perfect the blending of colours, it is possible to go back to change areas with which you may not be happy. The beauty of this technique lies in the powdery quality and that rules out any sealants.

Accessories

The table with its turned legs was a junk-shop find which was in a very sorry state. Gentle stripping and a good scrub revealed a battered but characterful table. An occasional polish with Cobra White Floor Wax is all we ever give it – with satisfactory results.

The crackled cupboard was painted inside and out in Plascon Computacolor Jumbunna Orange T69-5, Polvin. Brush stripes were painted onto the outer frames of the doors and a leafy stencil was applied across the doors in Strathmore Green (U79-4) from the Plascon Computacolor Chart, mixed in Plascon Polvin. The craquelure was created using Heritage Transfer Glaze as a first coat over the stencilled cupboard. This was left to dry overnight before a coat of Heritage Crackle Glaze was applied all over. Both of these are water-based, clear and translucent. As this last coat dries, you can see the craquelure appearing across the surface. Again it needs to be left overnight to dry thoroughly. Only then can the cracks be filled with some artist's oil paint to make them show up. Use a tiny bit on a piece of soft cloth; it can even be very slightly diluted with turpentine. Rub it into the cracks. Do not be tempted to use artist's acrylic paint as this will wipe off your crackle glaze! We used a creamy white mixture which shows up gently against the ruddy and green hues. All excess paint must be wiped away to leave only the cracks obviously coloured.

The fabric has a pleasant history. A dear friend of ours bought a country hotel in a fruit and wine area. We helped her to decorate the refurbished "lodge" and in the process decided to have new dining room curtains. Exactly how it came about we cannot recall, but it was decided that we would design some fabric for the curtains. The thought of a repetitive motif led us to the idea of stencilling. Once the design was stencilled as a prototype, we had to produce colour separations and these were duly passed on to the textile printing studio at the Cape Technikon. Our first printing was so terribly bad colour-wise that we almost gave up the idea. With some inspiration from a beautifully hued Liberty fabric we selected new colours – and could hardly believe the difference.

Should you, however, want to produce just a few metres of fabric, it is not a bad idea to simply stencil it by hand. Refer to the chapter on stencilling (page 115).

Neutrals

*The natural wood of a settee, the "limed" table, antique woodgrained tins
and calico curtains are set against walls textured in a gentle Plascon Beige Tan
(M54-1). The coir matting provides a superb base for this
sepia-neutral mise en scène.*

In the introduction we mentioned that beige in the nineties is quite different from the dead beiges of the sixties. Here we have an example. Our walls were distressed using Beige Tan (M54-1), a versatile colour which is neither beige, tan nor ochre but which combines these hues and changes in different lights: in shade it is beige, in sunlight ochre and in electric light it is tan.

A neat white Polvin surface was prepared for the distressing – and that is exactly the way one would describe the first step of the process. Moisten a marine sponge in water and squeeze it out well. Put a few tablespoonfuls of full-strength Polvin Beige Tan into an enamel plate or painting tray. Pick up some of this Polvin with your sponge. It is very easy to overload the sponge, which makes it imperative to dab the excess off onto the edge of the plate, or better still, onto newsprint where you can see the imprint as well. Sponge across the wall at random, closely at times and sparsely otherwise, always dabbing very lightly and turning the sponge fractionally before each dab. This prevents rows of regular patterns forming. The texture must not be even. A rather odd, measly appearance evolves, but do not despair …!

The next step requires a glaze to be mixed: equal parts of Plascon Water-based Glazecoat, Clear Matt, and Plascon Polvin Beige Tan. Rub this glaze over the sponged walls. Move slowly across the wall, vigorously rubbing small areas at a time and making sure that all edges are rubbed out, i.e. softened in order not to leave marks caused by the quickly drying glaze. As the glaze is applied over the sponging it softens automatically. A second rubbing is always advisable – it softens the effect even more and adds subtlety. While it is a lot of extra work, you will be rewarded with a professional-looking room if you pay special attention to the edges and corners and brush the glaze right up to the very limit at all times.

Beautiful sprig and toile de jouy fabrics have been combined to make up a bed throw. Their browny-beige colours complement each other and brown piping finishes off an otherwise simple design. Brown and canvas checked cushions and tablecloth continue the colour theme. Rather monotone, the whimsical combination of checks, sprigs and toile de jouy remains interesting. It is in fact a good example of "beige in the nineties".

The table is an ordinary modern pine table of pleasant proportions. It has been given a faux limed effect. Originally furniture was treated with lime to protect it against dry rot and beetles. At the same time it provided a decorative aspect. Because of the toxic qualities of lime and the advent of excellent anti-beetle products, liming fell into disuse. The only available product resembling the traditional method is Liming Wax by Liberon, an expensive imported commodity worth every cent. We would not hesitate to apply this fine product and finish to sophisticated oak furniture. On the other hand, we would think twice about faking the effect on such pieces using emulsion paints.

We provide three options for liming wood. Various artists develop their own techniques and we want to make it quite clear that there are many, many ways to reproduce this and other effects.

Because the fundamental endeavour is to lodge lime in the grain and recesses of the wood, you have to ensure that the grain is open and receptive. All surfaces must, therefore, be free of varnish, polish or other agents that would resist the lime. Clean raw wood is what is prescribed and if there is any doubt that the grain is clogged or closed, apply a fine wire brush to the wood, brushing in the direction of the grain. Take care not to gouge ruts with too rough a brush. Follow up with a gentle sanding with 120-grit glasspaper to get rid of loose hairy fibres.

In the most refined method, Liming Wax by Liberon is applied using very fine steel wool – not the household type but a specialist kind used by cabinet-makers and restorers. The fragrant white paste is applied into all recesses and over all surfaces. The piece of furniture appears to be wearing a bad face pack. But the reward comes when you polish off the excess wax, using Cobra White Floor Wax on a cloth, and buff it up with a soft cloth. A soft veil of white remains, with the recesses and grain picked out stronger. The fragrance of pure turpentine lingers and the wood is smooth to the touch.

In keeping with current fashion in décor, you can tint liming wax by dissolving very small amounts of artist's oils in the required colours in pure turpentine and adding it to the wax. Refrain from using too much turpentine and creating a runny paste.

A very easy but effective method of faking liming is to dilute three parts of Plascon White Polvin with one part of water. This is wiped or brushed onto the raw, clean wood and wiped off, leaving the desired whiteness behind. Repeat the process if it is not strong enough; if it is too white you can leave it to dry and then sand away as much as you want to.

Should you anticipate varnishing the surface, it is advisable to create a much whiter surface than is necessary because the varnish "swamps" the colour to give it translucency. This method is particularly suitable for modern pine furniture, but remember to request unvarnished pieces when purchasing. Any colour can be used, but bear in mind that a coat of varnish will change the colour. Whites turn yellow and blues go green while other colours are affected in a lesser way. Plascon markets an Oil-based Glazecoat (CV82) which does not modify colours. It remains clear and dries with a gloss finish. To counteract the gloss, should you prefer a matt finish, we advise you to apply three consecutive coats of CV82, allowing proper drying in between. Once the surface is bone dry it can be sanded with very fine paper (no coarser that 120-grit!). It is rather worrying to see the surface turning a dull grey, but you subsequently polish it with some Cobra White Floor Wax and buff it up with a soft cloth. You will be astonished by the lovely soft patina!

We receive countless enquiries regarding the limewashing of floors. The basics above apply in every respect: work on clean, raw wood, use diluted emulsion (PVA) paints for

washes and full-strength emulsion for stencils or hand-painted borders. There are many patent sealers on the market but we like to use Plascon Glazecoat Gloss or Matt. Three coats should seal a floor sufficiently to withstand two years of traffic before it requires another sealing.

A third way of creating a limed finish is to use a varnish, Plascon Woodcoat Suede (X44) or Gloss (X33), as a medium. Some Titanium White artist's oil colour must be dissolved in a little turpentine before it is added to the varnish. It depends on how white you want the wood to be, and too much Titanium White in this mixture will certainly inhibit the translucency. Stir the oil colour in gently; do not shake the varnish up as this will cause bothersome air bubbles in the varnish. Since this mixture dries rapidly and since varnish is very tacky, speed and determination are prerequisites. The eventual effect is really good but nonetheless superficial. Discoloration is also inevitable.

A most effective way of creating a lime-washed surface relies on the combination of translucency and opacity obtained from diluted undercoat.

The wood to be limed must either be new and untreated or stripped and cleaned of paint, varnish and oils. Combine one part of Plascon Universal Undercoat – Merit and one part of mineral turpentine. Paint this mixture onto a section of the wood, working it into the grain. While it is still wet all superfluous undercoat mixture must be wiped away with an absorbent lint-free cloth. You can regulate the amount of white left in the grain and recesses. Work in areas small enough to cope with before it dries. Leave a wet edge to facilitate a smooth finish.

Finishing could involve a thorough waxing with white floor wax or two coats of Woodcoat Suede (X44) (this could cause yellowing) or two coats of Oil-based Glazecoat (CV82). This is quite glossy but does not yellow with age.

Please bear in mind that when you varnish your finished product you will lose some of the whiteness so it is a good idea to retain enough white to counteract this phenomena.

The beautiful old spice tins are very special in respect of their original painted finishes which are well preserved. Both are wood-grained in the traditional manner. The flat oval tin was obviously pressed and factory-made – a utility object – but lacked the character of the traditional wooden spice box; therefore it was painted with a woodgrain finish. These were the norm.

A modern version of such woodgrain would require an initial coat of red, water-based, metal primer (Anti-Rust Coating) to cover the tin. Subsequently you make a thick creamy mixture of powdered paint (Raw Umber powdered tempera as used at school) and water with a drop of household detergent (dishwashing liquid) to facilitate mixing. This is brushed onto the dry red primer and flogged with a flogger (a very long and soft bristled brush). Rapidly beat the surface of the wet paint while moving the brush away from you. The resulting texture resembles a fibrous woodgrain with the red peeping through. Do small areas at a time and do not handle the dry parts unnecessarily. Once dry, the whole must be given a coat of Woodcoat Polyurethane Varnish – Suede (X44). Prepare an oil-based glaze using one teaspoon of turpentine, one tablespoon of Plascon Scumble Glaze and approximately 5 cm of Van Dyck Brown artist's oil paint squeezed from the tube! Use this mixture to drag a linear texture over the entire surface, bit by bit. This will simulate the grain of the wood but must not hide the fibrous texture underneath. Refer to examples of actual wood to discover the graphic aspect. Also try to select a brush according to its texture to get the striations the way you want them. Leave overnight to dry before you finally varnish the whole with Woodcoat Polyurethane Varnish – Suede (X44).

White and gold

White crispness! Somehow it can also be daring to stick to white. In this tranquil setting with its romantic touches the walls were neatly marked out and stencilled in gold, using crowns and fleur-de-lis. A delicate warped table was painted in white Velvaglo, as was the clock base. An oil-gilded ostrich egg, water-based-gilded star, the mercury glass and gilt-edged glass vases conclude the gold theme. Pure white drapery can easily be whipped off to be laundered!

Soft tones of white contrasted with gold produce a gentle romantic interior. The room was painted white before it was marked out in a regular square grid on a 45-degree angle. Once the size of the square has been decided on, a template can be cut from cardboard and simple dots can be made to determine the exact spots for the stencils. A spirit level will help to keep both vertical and horizontal lines straight.

Please refer to the chapter on stencilling (page 115) to find the recipe for making stencil paper. We decided to cut a crown and a fleur-de-lis stencil. These were arranged alternatively and stencilled using a stencil brush and Plaka Rich Gold. With such a stencilled wall one does not need to have pictures or strongly patterned fabrics. We decided to preserve the simplicity: the chair was draped with plain white cotton while the window drape is a fine voile with a fleur-de-lis pattern printed in white.

Accessories

The little table with its two drawers is a handy, rather elegant piece of furniture made out of various woods and consequently warped! Simply painted in white Plascon Velvaglo (Satin Sheen Enamel) it adopts graces above its station!

The star is moulded resin which has been gilded. We put them to various uses: a row of them stuck to the wall below a cornice enhances a high wall; attached to hooks on either side of a window they serve as hold-backs; on a dinner table they are decorative as napkin weights.

The gilding process is described in a separate chapter. Bear in mind that Wundasize takes perfectly on resin and you can therefore follow the steps as set out on page 104.

Black and white

The magic of black and white lies in the fact that neither ever presents itself as just a boring flat colour. One always finds a glint in black glass, a grain in wood sprayed black, a contour on a chair upholstered in white …

Our setting here had a bad wall as its main concern. After much deliberation it was decided to use 60 cm square boards, to texture them with Polycell Ripple and then to rub them with a very slight black glaze. Although they were simply nailed to the wall, studs on each corner add a finishing touch.

Sample boards become tired, scratched and ugly with age and we had a number of these hardboard squares. They were all selected or cut to be the same size throughout. Since they were badly damaged or textured frequently, we decided to use Polycell Ripple to apply a similar texture to all of them. For this we used a plastic spatula and instead of "ripples" we did "swirls". We painted a generous coat of Ripple onto each board and then dragged the spatula through it, forming arcs of fan shapes. We left them to dry lying down.

We were fortunate in that we had a wooden wall to nail them to, but steel pins will no doubt secure them to a plastered wall. These nails were limited to one per corner.

Only when they were secured to the wall, did we glaze them. Use a base of one cup of Plascon Glazecoat and about three teaspoons of black Polvin as a water-based glaze to rub onto the squares. We treated each one individually, creating contrasts of more or less shading. As the glaze was drying we wiped the tops of the texture to reveal the white base. After the first board we had misgivings, but as the numbers grew, the effect became evident and in fact quite stunning. Somewhere in a toolbox we found some 20 mm metal studs − old and oxidised, yet they were ideal to nail into the corners, ostensibly holding everything together but in fact only supplying the final touch!

Accessories

The table (page 62) is a hollow-core door resting on a set of iron legs. Three coats of white Velvaglo onto the raw – but well-sanded – wood of the top produced a really fine finish.

An old African clay pot stands elevated upon an Art Deco glass base. The table lamp was produced by Marlene Wyser Interiors, the glass beads sewn onto the shade adding a whimsical touch. The chair, upholstered in sailcloth, has an interesting ticking-piped edge. A piece of black-and-white silk draped over the chair is a remnant bought in 1970 and it still looks fashionable. The curvaceous chest of drawers is not really black but ebony in colour. As a sculptural piece it forms an excellent contrast to the rigid background, but its curves are echoed in the chairback and the table legs.

Marbling

*These marble panels are formal in shape but the style of painting is very casual.
Outsized diagonal marble patterns are pure fantasy and strongly contrasting hues
lend some drama to this study. The desk is painted green and has an antique patina
while the work surface is polished wood. Strong ethnic pattern underfoot brings
about an intriguing disparity of styles.*

The fantasy marble featured in our main photograph was executed in water-based glazes. With their rapid drying one is forced to work boldly and quickly, resulting in these graphic and pronounced panels.

A smooth base of Plascon Polvin or Double Velvet in white is required to begin with. Although our quest is for a fanciful result, the idea of panels, a "marble tradition", persisted. It is quite easy to measure out panels. Keep their sizes manageable and do not hesitate to mark them out in fine pencil lines. We find our spirit level of immeasurable help in obtaining neat shapes. Since the central panels are done first they are the ones to be taped out with detacked masking tape. A waterbased glaze is mixed using one part of Polvin in your choice of colour (we used Beige Tan M54-1) and two parts of Plascon Water-based Glazecoat Clear Matt. Using a 50 mm paintbrush (well used if possible so that the tip is tapered), we applied the glaze in diagonal bands, thinly at times and boldly elsewhere. You can even leave the base colour to show through here and there as a contrast. Turned on its side the brush will produce slender veins of some intensity. If you are quick enough you can even create an extra texture by ragging off some of the glaze before it dries. Keep it simple to start with,

though; once everything is dry you can always apply more glaze creating a layered effect.

Marble patterning can be problematic: you will have to look at marbles and practise until you have developed your own style of representing it. Your creativity will guide you provided you have the determination.

Once the central panels are dry, the masking tape can be removed and re-used to tape up the "frames". A similar glaze (Glazecoat and Polvin) in a contrasting colour is used for this. We selected a rusty-red Plascon Polvin Standard Colour (Ascot Tan) as a rather dramatic foil. Again the glaze is floated across the surface to form the marble patterning.

Since the glaze contains Glazecoat it is not necessary to seal these surfaces on walls. Furniture painted in this way, especially if it is used frequently, would need two finishing coats of Woodcoat (X44) or something similar.

Simple grey marble can be achieved easily, provided you follow basic steps and practise them. Once you are acquainted with the basics you can venture into variously coloured marbles and even produce fantasy marbled finishes of merit in modern interiors.

1. We remember so well the day we started our first course of marbling in a fascinating studio in a small English village. Suddenly we were confronted with an array of tools and media the likes of which we had never encountered before! One of them was a particularly soft and beautifully coloured brush, obviously well looked after. It had a baby sibling with a metal ferrule (the holder for the bristles). They are the badger softeners featured here with other marbling tools … an enamel plate, an ordinary 50 mm brush, a jamb duster (also called a hoghair softener), a marine sponge, a feather and some cloth. The tubes of paint are artist's oils in three colours: Davey's Grey, Payne's Grey and Titanium White. Needed but not shown here are mineral turpentine, raw linseed oil and Plascon Terebine Driers.

Prepare a mixture called film former or megilp using one part of raw linseed oil, two parts of mineral turpentine and the tip of a teaspoon of Plascon Terebine Driers. Do not make up a vast quantity; a few tablespoonfuls will do to start with. For all practical purposes you must work on a perfectly smooth Velvaglo Satin Sheen Enamel surface – white in this case. Moisten a lint-free cloth with some film former and rub a film of this megilp onto the surface to be painted. The area must not be swamped in oil! Prepare an area of approximately 500 mm². Thus you can manage all the various steps before the glaze dries out. Work in irregular shapes rather than in exact squares. That way stop-and-start areas will not be detectable.

Now pipe a little of each of the oil colours onto the edge of the plate. Pour a little film former into the centre of the plate. Use any ordinary 25 mm or 50 mm brush to mix some Titanium White, Davey's Grey and film former into a pale grey, single-cream consistency. This is called a glaze: it is translucent because it has an oily base, and opaque because of its pigment content.

Proceed to "fidget" – in a nervous manner(!) – some of this grey across the prepared surface. We tend to use a slightly diagonal movement because it provides movement and "marble always goes somewhere …" The movements must be spontaneous, natural and rather impulsive. Repeat these brush-marks using darker mixes or combinations of Payne's Grey, Titanium White and film former. Leave quite a lot of the white background untouched.

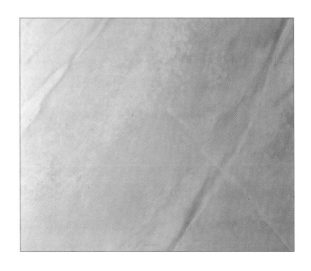

2. Now try your hand at stippling. Hold a jamb duster almost the way you would hold a pen. Pounce the dry bristles onto the newly glazed surface to blend the hues and tones somewhat and also to create a soft gritty texture throughout. As soon as the bristles become laden with glaze it is advisable to wipe them with a clean cloth. By stippling you pick up some glaze and deposit some. The film of megilp facilitates this, and if you want to move pigment across the surface you can tilt the jamb duster a little and pounce sideways to slide the colour along. End by stippling over the surface again for good measure.

3. Moisten your fingers lightly in film former and wipe them on a clean lint-free cloth. Do this a number of times; not to saturate it but to oil it slightly. Twist it into a loose rose shape and dab or roll it lightly across the stippled surface, just here and there and quite sparingly.

4. At this stage we start using the badger softener. Flick the soft bristles ever so lightly over the entire painted surface, literally softening the image. No brushmarks should show. Some craftsmen call this "knocking it back" – as if a gentle film is formed over the entire surface and the images recede. The flicking or light brushing can be done in any direction, wherever it is needed. Note how the softener is held for maximum comfort and effect.

5. Moisten a natural sea sponge in water and squeeze it out as best you can. Pour a moderate quantity of film former into a shallow dish. Pick some film former up with your sponge but dab it on the edge of the plate to get rid of any excess before you sponge the film former onto parts of the background area.

Watch closely to see what occurs when your film former (a solvent) opens up the glaze. It is magical! Before it opens up too much you have to badger the surface, collecting excess film former and softening the effect. Up to this stage it is evident that you have created a lovely stone look and this is as far as one would take it for this purpose. One could then obviously use various stone colours.

6. Veining is not easy and takes a lot of practise as well as conscious studying of actual marble. There are as many ways of representing veining as there are examples in nature. Try, though, to avoid regular repetition! Dip the feather in some glaze which is darker than the marble generally. Cut it spontaneously across the surface, sometimes going quite straight and sometimes moving sideways jerkily or pushing the feather to force it to open up. Whatever, the movements must be free and natural. Do not overdo the number of veins to start with.

7. Use the small badger to soften these veins.

8. Use a fitch (flat artist's brush) moistened with film former to cut right through some areas, preferably adjoining the veins, right down to the white background. These areas have to be softened with the badger.

9. Finally you need to finish off by giving the panel a neat frame. Gently mark out a frame all the way around the edge of the panel. You can use a pencil and if it's done lightly the line can stay there as a permanent delineation. Lay a strip of 80-grit sandpaper (± 50 mm wide) face down on the work that will be preserved, but lined up with the drawn line. Wipe the outer edge clean of all glaze using a cloth slightly moistened with film former. A very neat edge will result and you can continue wiping this way right around. It is most rewarding to watch a marble panel taking shape in this manner.

Stone finish

Two well-worn Lloyd Loom chairs were given bright floral cushions in this otherwise monochromatic setting. The shapes of roughly hewn stone blocks were demarcated with masking tape and then painted with water-based glaze. The cement pot was glazed in similar fashion but in darker tones. Coir matting provides durable textured flooring which harmonises closely with the background.

*A*wall painted in white Polvin would be the ideal surface to work on. If a regular finely hewn stone block design is required you would use masking tape attached to the wall in regular horizontal lines demarcating the blocks. Bear in mind that masking tape can pull the paint from the wall. Get accustomed to detacking the tape before taping up: stick it to your clothes or carpet and pull it off to diminish its tackiness before you use it on the painted surface.

We decided to recreate roughly hewn stone blocks and taped the rough blocks out. As we went along we tore each strip of tape in half lengthways and repasted them with their straight edges together. This way a rough, meandering line suggests the plaster between the blocks. Once the wall has been taped out the colour can be applied.

Mix a glaze using one part of Plascon Glazecoat Clear Matt and one part of Plascon Polvin Beige Tan (M54-1). Use a synthetic bath sponge to apply the glaze over the entire wall and work systematically from one block to another, creating lighter areas with the white of the base coat showing through and darker areas of glaze dabbed on thickly. Take care not to cause drips, though. It is a good idea to create a strong gritty texture by dabbing the sponge into the wet glaze before

you start the next block. At this stage the wall still appears rather anaemic – but it needs a second colour. Mix another glaze using one part of Plascon Glazecoat Clear Matt and one part of Brown Gold Polvin (D61-8).

Apply this second glaze just like the first one, creating a stronger mottled texture. As soon as the whole wall is done, the tape can be removed. The white lines now revealed need to be treated. Use some of the second glaze and rub and dab over all these lines. Do not be concerned about it spilling onto the blocks. Simply soften these spills with your sponge. Standing back you now become aware of the darker edges of the blocks – almost as if they bulge out and display rounded edges.

We have used only two colours but it could be interesting to use more. The blocks can also have different colour accents – as if they are not all from one part of the quarry.

For deeper coloured walls you could start on a darker background and work even darker. This is exactly the way we do *trompe l'oeil* tiles.

They can be painted on raw cement floors provided the cement is dry or preferably quite mature. Clean wooden floors – new and without any varnish or polish – would also be an option.

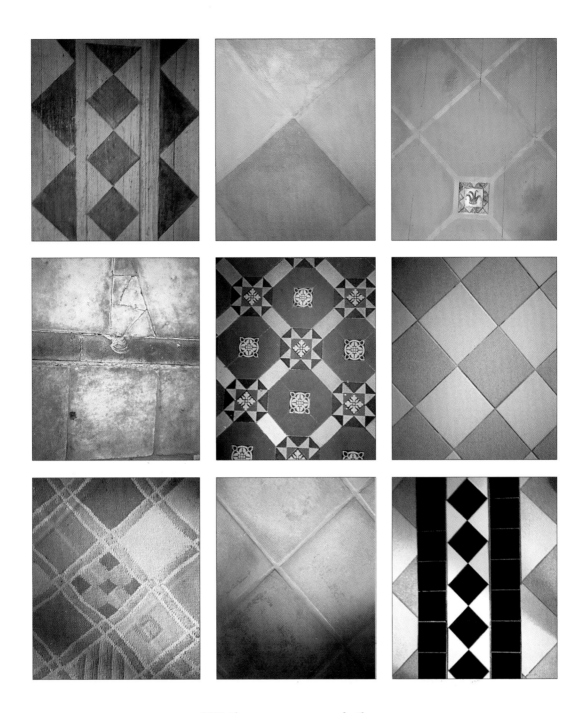

Floor tiles

This "tiled" floor is in fact nothing more than painted hardboard! Each tile is individually painted, dark around the edges to resemble some dimension and with a small handpainted tile at regular intervals. A bird bath is suitably rubbed with a mixture of a terracotta Polvin and Water-based Glazecoat (REF. 1125). Previously sporting badly chipped paint, the chair was sandblasted to reveal a lovely rusty patina which has been preserved by using several coats of Woodcoat Polyurethane Varnish (X44).

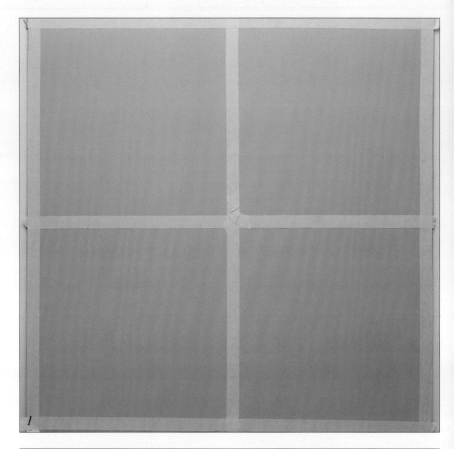

Floor tiles:
Step by step

1. Brush or roll a base coat of Plascon Wall and All (Standard Colour: Sand) onto the entire floor surface. This in itself is already a most tenacious surface.

Now measure out the tiles across the entire floor. A chalk line and a friend to help are two essentials. The design can be a challenge but looking at actual tiled floors − even at the tile merchants − can be most rewarding. Once all the lines are chalked out, you can tape out the floor with masking tape. Choose your own width but rather use one that is narrower than 22 mm.

2. An inset can be taken into account when the floor is taped up − a neat square where the four tiles meet, every second crossing.

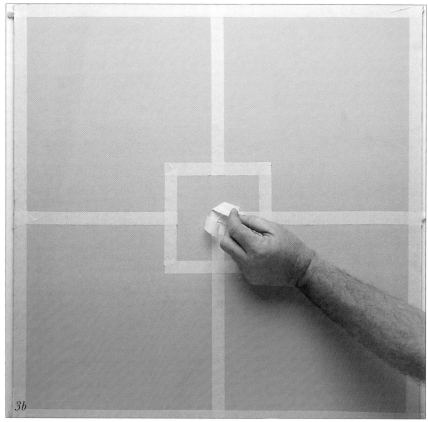

3. Use a craft knife (NT cutter or Stanley knife) to cut the crossed tape from the centre of the square.

4. Use a water-based glaze (one part Plascon Glazecoat Clear Matt with one part Polvin Ascot Tan Standard Colour) on a synthetic bath sponge to rub and dab a deeper translucent colour onto the tiles. Paint one tile at a time and concentrate some darker tone along the edges. This provides a gentle "cushioned" look. Cut the colour across the corners so that they will eventually appear slightly rounded rather than rigidly squared according to the sharp corners formed by the masking tape.

5. Paint the small tile inset in a contrasting colour. We used white Polvin but any colour can be used to complement the interior. A hand-painted motif in a blue Polvin finished our floor off, but a stencilled pattern or simple distressed colour could also look very good. Work in Polvin or acrylics.

6. Remove the tape and rub some of the Ascot Tan glaze over the "grouting". Spill onto the tile by all means but keep the inset clean and soften the edges of this rubbing. This will enhance the form of the tiles.

Finally, three coats of Plascon Glazecoat Clear Matt can be rolled over the entire floor. Although Glazecoat dries very fast, do be quite certain that one coat is dry before the next one is rolled on. As a sealant on Polvins, Glazecoat will not change the colours and will last at least two years before a repeat performance will be necessary.

Antiquing

This combination of ethnic artefacts from various origins required the walls to be painted in a primitive, basic way. We regarded the white bagged brick walls as too harsh a background and chose to simply rub them in a "brown" rudimentary to most cultures. The wall hanging is a raffia-and-rag weaving from Madagascar, the tall basket and the table are Oriental, the pot and carved lion are African, the khelim Middle Eastern and the chair a 1940s sidewalk bargain upholstered in a too expensive French leopard print velour!

Antiquing a white wall

The walls were given a good base coat of Plascon White Polvin. At this stage they must be well painted, flawless and ostensibly at the finished stage.

A brown glaze has to be mixed using Plascon Water-based Glazecoat Matt (REF. 1125) and Buffalo Universal Stainer (Brown). The proportions are largely dependent on how deep you want the hue. Do not mix up litres of glaze. Start with no more than one litre of Glazecoat for an average room. Even this might prove to be too generous. Add measured amounts (teaspoons) of Universal Stainer. Write down your quantities in case you need to repeat the mixture. Test your glaze in an inconspicuous spot and wipe it off with a wet rag or sponge as soon as you can. Do remember that the Universal Stainer is a very concentrated pigment and small amounts go a long way.

We used an ordinary round synthetic bath sponge (five-in-a-pack from the local supermarket) to do the rubbing. A piece of absorbent cloth would also be suitable. Work in random patches but aim at rubbing the edges out, i.e. thin the colour out at the edges until the sponge is dry. Do not be too ambitious when you load the sponge with glaze. Rather use a little frequently. It is much better to mix a lightly pigmented glaze and suffer two rubbings than to slap on a thick coat of unmanageable dark glaze.

An important detail very often neglected is the finishing off at the skirting and the cornice. Keep a brush handy to fill in at these areas. Pick up a tiny bit of glaze and run the brush along the cornice or skirting board. Fade this edge into the painted wall by rubbing it out with either the brush or the dry sponge. It is also easier to use a brush to finish off the corners. A sponge tends to cause blotches on the adjoining wall when you try to get into the corner. Spend time and patience finishing off a rubbed wall. This slightly darker frame distinguishes between a hastily done amateurish finish and the work of art that will elicit respect and admiration.

Verdigris

The refined tones of verdigris are demonstrated in this still life. In the background a wreath made in brass and chemically oxidised displays a spotty but subtly toned texture. The plant pot and boxes are sponged in Polvins but are similarly textured. A gold-leaf edge finishes the terracotta pot.

An old, insignificant turned wooden box is painted in various tones of a slightly differently hued verdigris. Brushmarks have been softened and the finished box was finally polished with Cobra White Floor Wax and buffed.

During our stay in Newent, Gloucestershire, we came upon a small family-run glassworks. We bought a few turquoise-spotted glass baubles only to discover that this family used to live in Bergvliet, Cape Town! These baubles reminded us of verdigris and are featured in our photograph to contribute towards a clean, crisp and tranquil composition.

Verdigris: Step by step

The literal translation of verdigris is green-grey. In general decorator's terms it has acquired a much wider significance. Referring to the colour of oxidised copper or brass one involuntarily thinks of a particular turquoise-green-grey colour. When one actually takes the trouble to look for naturally oxidised copper, the range of colours is astounding. They vary from brilliant turquoise-blue to slightly off-white and from yellow-green to black-turquoise. Decorators are currently using these colours and effects on a large scale and in many innovative ways. Shop counters, columns, panelled walls, outdoor furniture, plant pots, lamp bases and such are finished in verdigris and beautifully integrated into interiors. It has in fact become quite difficult to distinguish between the real and the faux. Here and there one still sees an old building with brass or copper trimmings or even an odd roof of bronze, while monuments often sport a lovely old verdigris-bronze patina. Some contemporary metal craftsmen jealously guard their secrets of instant chemical oxidation and painters reproduce the look with their paints.

1. Our demonstration is on a small wooden box but the same technique can be applied to cover walls, furniture, floors or wherever it can be used to advantage. In order to render some impression of copper as the base of verdigris we apply a Plascon Polvin in a standard colour called Ascot Tan. It is painted straight onto the wood.

Should you want to paint onto metal, it is advisable to prime – and therefore seal – it properly with a metal primer followed by a solid coat of Plascon Merit Universal Undercoat. The metal will then be ready for a coat of Ascot Tan Polvin.

2. The vibrant turquoise we apply next is a Plascon Computacolor called Rowena (M42-5). We elected to sponge the colour on. For this we used a natural marine sponge which, just before it is used, is dipped into water and then squeezed out thoroughly. Spoon some of the Rowena PVA into an enamel plate or a paint tray. Pick up a modest amount of paint, literally just touching the surface with the sponge. Dab it onto the edge of the plate to distribute the paint and to make sure that it is not overladen. Sponge gently onto the painted box, creating a light texture which you can build up. Do not work too evenly and allow some of the base colour to show through.

3. It is important to add a different hue to create more interest. We selected a yellow-green colour called Freedom Green (38-12D) of a similar intensity and sponged it freely on parts of the box, fading on and off. Other options for colour at this stage could be Plascon Polvin Mod Blue or Mod Yellow added to the Rowena. Experiment and have fun!

4. Finally, you can sponge the faintest scatter-

ing of white touches onto the box. This represents the white powdery aspect of actual verdigris. The matt appearance of this technique is so typical that we do not advise a sealing coat of varnish. At the very most we would use a coat of Glazecoat, Matt (REF. 1125).

A point that needs to be cleared up is the choice of textures. We used a sponged texture. This is reminiscent of copper upon which water rained or dripped causing a spotty, pitted surface. A large plant pot might look good with the colours streaked on with a brush – as if rainwater has run down the sides. To take it even further you can dilute paint with water, load a sponge with it and squeeze it out along the top edge allowing it to dribble down the sides. You can leave these water marks to dry completely on their

own, but a stronger graphic quality is created by allowing them to dry partially before you wipe them clean of wet paint. The outer edges of the dribbles would have dried already, leaving clear fine lines delineating their path – resulting in a very attractive decorative finish.

The work surface of our pictures shows a much yellower and quite different verdigris effect. Here a base of Plascon Ascot Tan appears through various layers of turquoise and moss greens. These layers were painted on in succession with tones and hues changing subtly, coat after coat. We then sanded it down both in the direction of the brushmarks and across.

Consequently a beautiful weathered and distressed surface was created with all the greens as well as the Ascot Tan featuring.

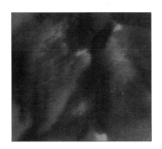

Tortoiseshell

Few techniques provide quite such an exotic touch as tortoiseshell. The colouring is rich and, worked on a yellow, red or gold background, acquires a depth that is most remarkable. Real tortoiseshell pieces are limited in size to the proportions of the sea turtle. This is now an endangered species, and real and particularly antique pieces are precious and expensive. If you intend copying nature, painting on small objects faking inlay would be appropriate. Diametrically opposed to this is the idea of painting walls or ceilings and cornices! A London firm doing such fittings refers to the technique as "beast"!

Our setting shows a quartered panel of tortoiseshell done on a strong yellow base. A wooden box has been gilded and the lid tortoiseshelled on the gold leaf. "Ebony" bands divide the tortoiseshell panels and relate to the treen vase.

The greatest advantage of faux finishes is their romantic aspect: you cannot pick up a few tortoiseshell trinkets from the local gift shop anymore, but the painted surface can take you back in time. When you cannot travel to exotic places, a painted tortoiseshell box will bring the exotic quality into your own home!

Tortoiseshell: Step by step

The technique we describe here is oil-based. Our requirements are: Raw Umber, Burnt Umber, Burnt Sienna and Van Dyck Brown artist's oil colours, film former (see recipe on page 71), a small badger softener, a large badger softener, a flat hoghair fitch and a marine sponge. The base we have chosen to work on is Plascon Velvaglo Parakeet mixed with a little white Velvaglo to tone it down. Being a fantasy finish, other possible base colours include Plascon Velvaglo Persimmon or Flamenco (Standard Colours), any yellow from pale to golden brown and even gold leaf (if you're feeling extravagant!).

Holding a piece of tortoiseshell against the light shows up its translucency – all those glowing honey, amber and treacle colours. To simulate these colours we use oil colours floated as glazes over the base colour. Pour some film former into an enamel dish, a little to begin with. Squeeze some Raw Umber artist's oil colour onto the edge of the plate. Use a piece of lint-free cloth to wipe a slight film of megilp (film former) over the area to be worked.

1(a). Mix some Raw Umber and megilp to a single-cream consistency. Proceed to dot the colour onto the oiled area. Create concentrated areas of these elongated dots and disperse them in other areas. Repeat the process with the other three colours in turn, working from light to dark. The megilp dilutes the oils, provides the translucency and helps to speed up the drying time. Stipple over the entire surface using a jamb duster or hoghair softener. To stipple, pounce the bristles onto

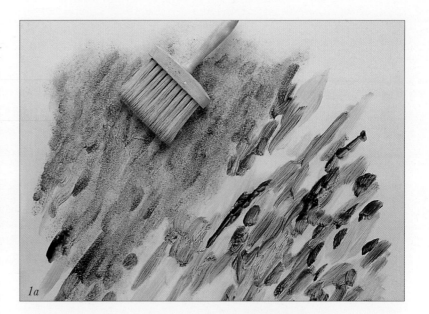

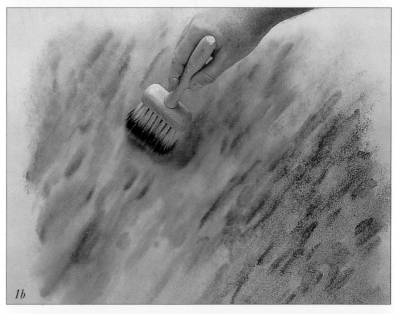

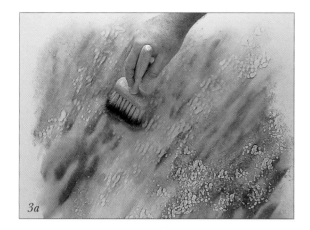

3a

3b

4a

4b

the glaze thus distributing or evening out the colour. Wipe the brush every now and then on a piece of cloth to remove the glaze that you have picked up on the top of the bristles. 1(b). Soften the surface gently by flicking the jamb duster over the surface of the glaze. Try not to leave any brushmarks.

2. Cissing is the interesting process of depositing solvents onto a glaze, causing it to open up and forming "holes" in the painted surface. This is how it is done: Moisten a marine sponge in water and squeeze it out very well. Pick up a modest amount of film former or megilp from the plate or paint it onto the sponge. Dab this first onto the edge of the plate to get rid of any excess and then into the wet glaze on your surface. A few discreet dabs will suffice. As you watch, the glaze is dissolved and it opens up. Overloading of the sponge can result in ugly big holes forming. As soon as you notice such, you should stipple over them; the jamb

duster will absorb the superfluous megilp.

3. The two badger-hair softeners have magical properties. Both can be softly flicked over the wet surface of a newly painted glaze, thus softening the appearance or creating depth. The smaller one, however, has shorter bristles and is well suited to move the glaze or slide it along. The larger one is essentially a softener and polishes a wet glaze to perfection. At this stage the two can be used in tandem to bring about a soft translucent tortoiseshell effect.

4. Finally, you can finish off the panel by wiping the edges. Cut a neat straight strip of 80-grit glasspaper. Measure out and mark off an outline for the panel. Place the glasspaper face down on the inside of the outline and rub away all the glaze outside the panel. Use a cloth with a little megilp on it. Continue all the way around the panel. Even after all these years the cleaning of edges still amuses and amazes us … suddenly amorphous colours become tortoiseshell!

Malachite

The natural lively patterns of malachite and the brightness of its hue are a never-ending inspiration for the painter. In our picture we feature a large panel as a background, but the traditional use of malachite is in small doses on boxes, lamp bases, etc. A French textile firm has, however, used large malachite patterns and colour to inspire a fabric print. They even have a range of colourways.

Somehow the colour is "modern" and it is often teamed with the other brights and white. We opted for a contrasting reddish brown and objects both modern and old, to create a timeless quality.

*T*he striations and undulating pattern of malachite have always fascinated us, but it is really the colour that bewitches us. Curio shops display malachite eggs, boxes, ashtrays and some other things that have very little purpose other than being resting places for flies! Familiarity with these often keeps us from really looking at the stone as such and enjoying the incongruous colour and pattern. One seldom sees very large pieces of malachite, and that is the reason for jewellers and lapidaries being very selective and using excellent fragments in jew-ellery and interesting composite obelisks, spheres and other shapes. Copying malachite on trinket boxes, picture frames and other small articles can be most amusing, but we are even more intrigued by the work of artists who give free reign to their spirits and, thus inspired, interpret large malachite shapes on furniture or even stretches of wall. They do not always use the natural colours: the most inventive being a French fabric, currently on the market, with a malachite pattern in the regular green with colourways in blue, rust and pink.

Our interpretation requires a Plascon Velvaglo Standard Colour by the name of Cucumber as a base to work on. We usually add a little bit of cobalt blue to this. Veridian Hue artist's oil colour is a brilliant green which suits our purposes well. A touch of Lamp Black artist's oil colour provides some depth.

Mix a glaze using a tablespoonful of Plascon Scumble Glaze, one teaspoon of turps and about 5 cm of Veridian Hue oil colour piped from the tube. Combine the turps and the oil colour before adding the scumble glaze. The resultant glaze should be nicely creamy.

Rub the surface to be painted with a cloth moistened with film former (megilp) to oil it

slightly. Paint on a thin layer of the green glaze. The simplest tool of all has to be fashioned at this stage: tear a piece of stiff card into a 7 cm strip that you can hold comfortably with the tips of your fingers. You can bend it before tearing it, but it must nonetheless be a rough tear. Use this as a scraper to scrape a path, undulating and stripy like the shapes in malachite, through the painted-on glaze. Tear a number of strips and use them alternately, filling the board with malachite shapes. Either wipe your piece of cardboard frequently or discard it when it gets clogged. The process is quick, simple and enjoyable. Finish by tidying up the edges (see Tortoiseshell: Step by step, page 96). This technique takes a long time to dry.

Gilding

Aunt Minnie, an eccentric dear, once came to Christmas dinner bearing a strange gift of her ebony elephant whose tusks kept falling out, bedecked with a tinsel bow. We immediately set about painting the elephant in Plascon's Mod Red Polvin. New at the game of gilding, we rubbed candlewax all over the surface and this acted as a primitive "size". Then we proceeded to gild the entire body using transfer gold, a thin leaf attached to tissue paper. One places it face down upon the sized object, rubs the back of it and in so doing transfers the gold to the size where it sticks.

*I*n our illustration Minnie's elephant is holding a gilt frame aloft. We use these modest frames to teach gilding at our courses. Eventually the students are more enthusiastic than we are and we sometimes wonder: will they also have gilt curtain rods, ceilings, African carvings and ball-and-claw furniture soon?

Gilding: Step by step

1. The object to be gilded in this case is a small wooden frame, painted in Plascon Mod Red Polvin. Assembled around the frame is a plain wooden frame, a piece of black velvet fabric, a dish of methylated spirits, one of baby powder, one of water-based gold size (Wundasize) and two samples of gilded battens – one on a black base, the other on "rouge". Finally there is a booklet of Dutch metal leaf interleaved with tissue paper. This is a substitute for gold leaf and therefore is much cheaper. It retains its lustre for ages and, being thicker, is easy to handle. There is a range of colours from silver to gold to bronze.

2. Wundasize is applied to the red-painted frame. Any base colour can be used but traditionally brick red, ochre, black and brown were *de rigueur.* Being water-based the product dries rapidly but, at the same time, retains its tackiness for days. Traditional gold size is oil-based, takes a long

104

time to dry to the required tackiness and leaves only a few hours for the gilding process itself. The brush can be cleaned in methylated spirits and then in soapy water. Leave the "size" to dry from its initial milkiness to clear.

3. Gold leaf is very delicate and needs to be handled sandwiched between two sheets of tissue paper or lifted on a brush. Dutch metal leaf can be handled with your fingers provided you wear soft cotton gloves or dust your hands with baby powder or French chalk. Place sheets or sections of sheets of the Dutch metal leaf on the "sized" areas, pressing them down gently with the piece of velvet cloth. Cracks can be filled by dropping small fragments of leaf, known as "skewings", onto them and pressing them down onto the gold size. It is quite beautiful, however, if you allow some of the red to peep through cracks and holes. Continue covering the entire frame in the same manner.

4. Traditional gilding requires laborious burnishing but in this instance you are required to rub down the leaf with the velvet pad. This smoothens the surface and is the only way to push the leaf into the recesses.

If you are not averse to natural ageing (oxidising) in the distant future, you can leave the frame as is. A coat of clear gloss varnish would help to retain the splendour if that is preferred. Try Plascon CV82 Oil-based Glazecoat or Plascon Woodcoat X33 Gloss.

Lapis lazuli

Lapis lazuli has, through the ages, enchanted the world. The magical blues with their depth and, especially, the glint of gold inspired the artists of old to grind it up for a pigment of incomparable hue.

Lapis lazuli:
Step by step

For our exercise we rely on a water-based glaze and the left-over "skewings" (bits of gold leaf).

1. Our base coat is Plascon Polvin Betty Blue (M18-8 Computacolor) painted straight onto clean smooth bare wood. Two coats may be necessary.

2. The glaze we use is a mixture of one part of Plascon Water-based Glazecoat Matt (REF. 1125) and one part of Plascon Polvin Kepple Blue (T82-6 Computacolor). Take some of this mixture onto a natural sponge and sponge over the base coat, varying the intensity and depth of application.

3. While the glaze is still wet, drop some of the gold-leaf skewings onto the surface, pressing them down gently. A veined effect is created by dragging a fine artist's brush, wet with methylated spirits, through the glaze. Opening up can be achieved by dipping a stencil brush into methylated spirits and flicking it onto the wet glaze.

4. Once dry, two coats of Plascon Woodcoat Polyurethane Varnish – Suede (X44) are applied to finish off. Allow drying time between coats.

Crackling and craquelure

We must have stripped many a piece of furniture that should never have been stripped. It is only lately that we have discovered the charm of crackled paint, faded colour and, frequently, the vestiges of fine old bits of decorative painting on chests and other pieces. Many of these old pigments, historical works of art, have been destroyed in our haste to "restore". Somehow we just could not understand that we were in fact destroying patina and character that only years of being can impart. Now we search for unrestored, unspoilt pieces.

In our romantic quest for things of yesteryear, we paint faded walls, cracked stone and blistering woodwork. Crackling and craquelure

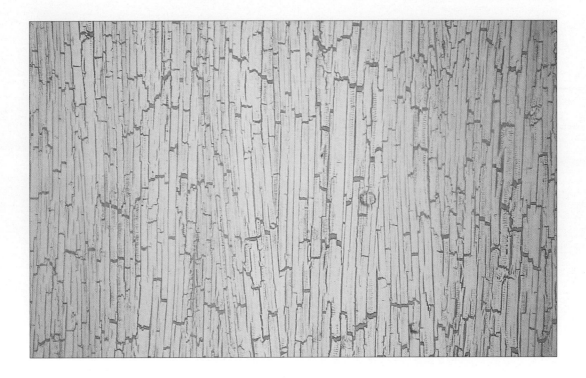

are techniques used for providing painted surfaces with not only a patina but also a surface texture to fake antiquity.

An easy way of crackling paint on woodwork gives instant results and never fails to amuse. Excellent on furniture, dados, door jambs, etc., it has become a decorative element in interiors ranging from peasant to posh.

Here is how we do it: Paint or stain wood in a strong or dark colour. We often stain new pine with Plascon Woodstain.

The next step is to paint the surfaces with Alcolin White Wood Glue (referred to in English publications as PVA). Treat small areas at a time; it might dry too quickly otherwise.

Immediately, while the glue is still wet, paint your paler contrasting colour over it, using a Polvin. Should you be in a hurry, direct a hair dryer onto your work. The cracks form as the Polvin dries before the glue does, and it all happens while you watch. Thickly applied glue will result in wide cracks. They also tend to form in the direction of your brushstrokes. Change brushes from time to time and rinse them in between to prevent a build-up of glue on your Polvin brush.

Once your piece of furniture has been crackled, it can be varnished (Woodcoat Polyurethane Varnish, Suede or Gloss or CV82). For a really fine patina you can rub an antiquing mixture over the surface, leaving more pronounced residues in nooks and crannies. A fine spattering of the same mixture can supply an array of fly spots.

We keep a bottle of antiquing mixture for use at any time: Mix together 7 cm of Raw Umber squeezed from a tube of artist's oil with a teaspoonful of turpentine. Dissolve the oil paint well before adding a tablespoonful of Scumble Glaze. This mixture has the consistency of single cream and the colouring of age. Rub or paint some of it into the surface you want to antique and, using a soft cloth, remove as much as you feel fit. This method works very well on Velvaglo and oil-glazed and varnished surfaces, but it needs an experienced hand on Polvins where it is absorbed before you can move it.

Another way of providing painted wood with a weathered look is to use a polyurethane varnish instead of the wood glue. It follows that a coat of Polvin – which is water-based – painted over a wet oily varnish would "open up" to reveal the wood under-

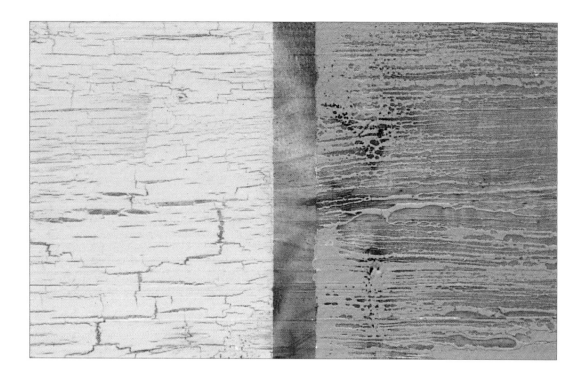

neath, leaving lovely cracked traces of paint. This technique requires a much longer drying time but has its own special charm.

There is also a way to recreate flaked paint on a wooden surface. Smear trickles and splotches of Vaseline onto the surface to be painted. Cover the lot with a coat of Polvin and leave it to dry. Use a dry cloth and rub through the paint, removing the Vaseline and paint in patches. Subsequent varnishing and antiquing conjures up romantic thoughts of days gone by …

China craquelure refers to the fine network of lines traced across the surface of a fine oriental piece. On paintings many coats of glaze over a canvas can age to cause fine crackling.

Another of our romantic indulgences, craquelure can be recreated with the aid of two Heritage products. These are not the only products or necessarily the best methods, but French and English imports are expensive … in which case you cannot do better. Acquire some Heritage Transfer Glaze and Heritage Antique Crackle. Both these products are water-based and translucent and we can only urge you to experiment with them to find the texture to satisfy you. Craquelure is a superficial, final treatment which means that you have to finish all your painting, stencilling, etc., before you crackle.

Paint a coat of Transfer Glaze over the article. Don't be too parsimonious, but don't slap it on either. Leave to dry overnight, making quite sure that it is bone dry. Proceed to paint a coat of Antique Crackle all over. Leave to dry well. If you hold it up against the light, you will discern the crackling forming, but face-on nothing will be evident.

The next step is of utmost importance. Use some antiquing mixture − remember that this is oil-based − on a soft cloth to rub into the cracks. This takes some effort and patience. Get the oil colour into all the cracks and then rub away the excess, dampening the cloth with a drop of turpentine if necessary.

The cracks can also be brought to light using a Plascon Scumble Glaze, oil colour and turpentine mixture of any colour other than Raw Umber. If you have an object painted in a dark hue, white cracks may be more visible. Never use a water-based colour to rub into the cracks − the Antique Crackle will dissolve and rub away and all your hard work will be in vain.

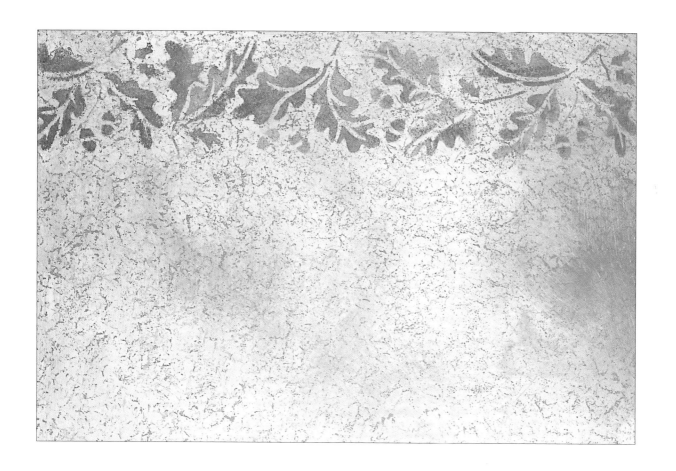

Stencilling

Stencilling, as the art of repetition, usually features bands of recurring motifs. This wall is a departure from this idea and was created using only two leaf stencils and hand-painted branches. Plascon's Mod Green and a brownish colour made up of Mod Red, Mod Yellow and Mod Green were used for the leafy stencil on a white wall. The harshness of this spectacle was daunting. However, three coats of Plascon Water-based Glazecoat mixed with Mod Green were rubbed over the entire wall, resulting in this ethereal garden scene.

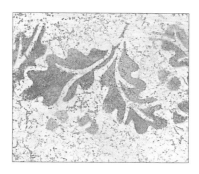

The raw cement floor (page 114) was painted streakily in Plascon Polvin's Ascot Tan and a mixture of Mod Green and Ascot Tan, and sealed with three coats of Water-based Glazecoat Matt (REF. 1125). The garden quality of the scene is enhanced by the introduction of a metal console bearing a leaf pattern which echoes that of the design on the wall. The see-through aspect of the table allows one to appreciate the wall motif which has been taken from skirting to cornice. Natural tones of brown in the orb, wooden bowl and antique books continue the theme.

Our first encounter with stencilling was through an American woman who had settled in Cape Town. Her fondness for American folk art, its many applications and permutations inspired us and, reading about it, we produced a small range of stencils. They were very much of the simple Shaker kind and since Christmas was near, we made hearts, stars, smiling moons, baubles, etc. Using a fret saw, we cut Christmas tree shapes from plywood, painted them deep green and stencilled spiky needles all over, superimposing the red heart, bow, star, moon and bauble stencils. The trees were provided with supports to enable them to stand up. Looking back we must admit that they were "crafty" and rather naive − yet that was exactly what they were supposed to be. Using stencils we were able to produce numbers of

these in a relatively short space of time. They sold well and we are happy to have kept one for our archives.

Stencilling concerns the repetition of a motif or design using a cutout pattern. Paint is applied through the cutouts and restricted to their limits. Let us look at making a stencil pattern and the use of it to produce a repetitive frieze. Many materials can be used to make stencils. As is our preference, we make our stencil card using a traditional oiled paper resembling parchment as follows: Mix five parts of Boiled Linseed Oil (one buys it as such from hardware stores) with one part of Plascon Woodcare Polyurethane Varnish and one part of mineral turpentine. The resultant

mixture is viscous and rather messy to work with. Place a thick wad of newspapers on a work surface and lay a sheet of 150 g Manilla paper on it. Use a brush to paint the oily mixture onto both sides. We prefer to do a number of sheets while the going is good. Manilla paper is the kind of stiff paper schoolchildren use for their projects. The colour is immaterial: it usually comes in white, pink, blue, green and yellow; rather a pastel lot. Once drenched in oil, these sheets must be left to dry. We sometimes peg them to the washing line (if the Southeaster is not blowing) or leave them to dry flat on more newsprint. Whatever, the drying time is long since oil dries slowly.

This paper is really a boon to the creative person. We frequently use it to make lampshades which, as they grow older and since they are drenched in linseed oil, acquire a deeper and richer tone but retain the superb translucency which is the most effective quality of parchment. It is not the only suitable material for stencils: the odd art and craft shop might stock commercially produced stencil parchment, one could use old X-ray plates or acetate, thin metal or whatever you feel happy with and which will produce the best results for you. Our concern with thin plastic materials is that they tend to bleed paint in underneath the stencil. Once this is understood their translucency may be of such importance to you that you will learn to cope with tricky cutting and bleeding paint. Translucency is important if you are producing a frieze, and spacing is vital. Should you use a parchment stencil, it is wise to cut a full motif, say a stem, leaves and bud, and to cut the tip of the stem starting a new pattern as well as the tip of the bud ending a previous pattern. To summarise: the stencil will then feature a tip of a bud, the full motif and finally a tip of the stem. Moving the stencil on, you would place the bud of the stencil over the stencilled bud, do the stencilling … and so on.

Finding a suitable design for a stencil need never be a problem. Motifs on fabrics can easily be transposed to a stencil, a favourite theme may produce a motif, nature can provide one, or these days one can simply buy them readymade from craft shops and paint dealers.

Working from an existing design, a fabric pattern or nature you first have to produce a line drawing or contour drawing. Make a photostat of this drawing and use a koki or similar pen to reduce the drawing further (draw over the copy) to a collection of planes separated by "bridges". These planes must be cut out using an artist's knife or scalpel and working on a cutting board. If the design, for instance, is of a daisy, you would cut out each petal separately, leaving a solid bridge separating one from the other. The centre may well be a simple round hole cut into the stencil.

Our next endeavour would be to do the actual stencilling. Again there are no hard-and-fast rules. Returning from England where we had been to attend some courses, we brought back a collection of stencil brushes and we consequently became addicted to them. To our astonishment a dear old friend of ours, Gerald Coetzee, looked disdainfully at our collection and, mumbling something that sounded like "You ain't seen nothin' yet!", presented us with two 300 mm stencil brushes!

They were the last of old, old stock from Hamiltons and Gerald knew about them. We were especially grateful to him for these when we executed some giant stencils on a ceiling.

In contrast to this, we have seen superb stencilling done with a piece of mutton cloth. A young woman, fresh from a top English design school and the workshops of a famous English painted-kitchen manufacturer, showed us how it is done. She cut fine stencils, rolled a piece of mutton cloth into a tight little ball and used very little paint to produce wondrous patterns. Other tools can be natural or synthetic sponges and old brushes with their bristles cut short.

Whatever the case may be, these tools have to transfer paint in very small quantities through the openings of the stencils onto the surface underneath. We prefer to use Polvin or artist's acrylics because they dry rapidly, which reduces the risk of smudging when one moves a stencil on. Oil-glazed surfaces and most eggshell enamels accept acrylic paints. Once dry, we varnish them for protection. A great English stencil connoisseur, Lyn Le Grice, uses cans of water-based spray paint – with the result that she has stencilled a house from top to bottom and produced a superb book on it!

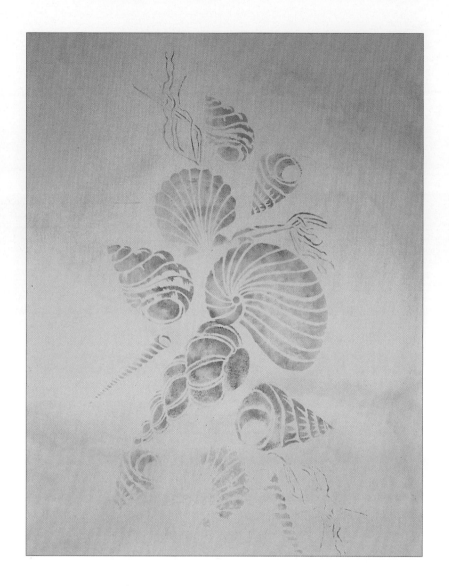

We enjoy our traditional ways and this is how we go about them. Set out paints in the way an artist would do it − either on a palette or in a tin plate. Secure your stencil in place using detacked masking tape or spray adhesive. Take a very modest amount of paint onto the brush, sponge or cloth and test it on a piece of clean paper. It must not be too wet, resulting in smudges. Dab the paint through the stencil with firm stabbing movements. Do not be tempted to paint through the stencil; this will cause an excessive build-up of paint under the stencil, causing bleeding. There is no remedy for this − only painstaking touching up or painting out.

We use more than one colour on one stencil, using one brush for a number of harmo-nious colours. Provided you use a very dry brush, changing colours is not a problem and taking one colour onto another could enhance the image. Some people cut a stencil for each colour − we don't because it diverts too far from the original idea of stencilling and tends towards airbrushing which is an art form in its own right.

One of our inspirational pictures features an overall stencilled wall which is both challenging and most effective. In this particular case the study walls were demarcated into panels, and these were duly stencilled in using masking tape to keep neat straight lines. A gentle mauve was used on a pure white Polvin (PVA) background. The panels were then filled in with the stencilled floral motifs, all of them

butting up against their neighbours. The pattern repeat is obvious and effective in creating an even quality. Finally the walls were repeatedly rubbed with Water-based Glazecoat tinted with yellow ochre tinter from the Polycell range. Soon the mauve quality changed to a bruised brownish colour, fascinating in its shadowlike appearance.

Another one of our inspirational pictures features a giant floral stencil with golden curlicues. If you compare this one with the study stencil, you will find that they are loosely related to the same fabric design! The large flowers were stencilled in various colours, all relative to the interior, along a wide curved band between the walls and the ceiling of an elegant dining room. Instead of a tightly repetitive pattern, the flowers and leaves were scattered randomly. The extraordinary result has people looking and looking ... vainly trying to find some repetitive aspect!

In the case of a pattern repeat we usually start in the corners of the room, working towards the middle. Sometimes it requires a lot of stretching, shrinking or filling-in to finish in the middle in a visually appealing way. There have been occasions when we have had to cut a special stencil to round off the pattern.

Stencils are the blessed equalisers of wonky old cornices. With experience one can eventually place stencils in such a way as to detract from the skewness of a wall, i.e. follow neither the line of the angled cornice nor a perfect horizontal; work in between ... deceive!

Evergreens

Some paint techniques have a long history and will most probably remain with us forever. Their colours may change, their textures may change, their prominence may be more or less, but sponging, dragging and ragging are the evergreens. Currently one seldom sees any one of these used on its own in a pure unadulterated form. Combinations are cleverly devised and freely executed − a sure sign that paint techniques have grown up.

This chapter will nevertheless describe the practical aspects of these techniques as well as some of their derivatives.

Sponging

A kind man once made a gallant effort to join our conversation at a moment when I had just mentioned that I was about to sponge some walls. "Oh!" he said, "how clever! You would then be able to fall against the wall without hurting yourself." Well, not quite … sometimes you might feel like bashing your head against your sponged walls in utter frustration, but let us prevent that …

The *mise en place* is simple; get together a paint tray or an enamel plate, some sheets of unprinted newspaper, a few plastic spoons, the paints you intend using … and the sponge.

The sponge we refer to is a natural or sea sponge. Unfortunately the sponges we find on our beaches are not suitable − treated sponges are imported from Greece or the Orient and, although they are expensive, they can and should last forever if they are well cared for. Wash them well in the way you would treat brushes.

Water-based or oil-based paint can be used depending on your requirements. Our preference is for Polvin (PVA) because they dry rapidly and a second or third sponging can be done immediately. Washing sponges in water is also much easier. The choice of colours for sponging is as crucial as in any other case. A rule of thumb is: pale sponging upon a darker background. Our most successful sponging ever was a soft grey-blue wall sponged over with a mixture of the original colour with white added. The delicate difference between the two tints of the same colour resulted in a subtle velvety texture. At the other end of the scale we encountered a bright pink wall, ham-handedly sponged in pillar-box red; a sad combination and an alarming interior. There also is no exception to the rule that two coats of sponging produce better results than a single coat. These could be two coats of one colour, of two shades or tints, or of two harmonising colours.

The way to go about it is to prepare the

base colour. It is best to paint the walls as well as you would for a final finishing coat.

Moisten the sponge in water (see how it grows!) and squeeze it out well. Do this before you use the sea sponge for any work. Spoon some full-strength paint into the paint tray or the enamel plate. Touch the surface with your sponge – do not overload it. Test the print on a piece of blank newspaper or roller towel. Evaluate the quantity of paint and the texture. If it makes blobs because there is too much paint on the sponge, dab some of it off on the paper before you start sponging the wall.

Most sponges have a variety of textures as you turn them around. Test these and select the most appropriate one for your purpose. Proceed to sponge in "figure-of-eight" movements, constantly changing the direction of the sponge. The idea is to eliminate any possible linear line-up of similar imprints which would stand out. One usually aims for an even distribution of texture but since this is a broken-colour technique, slight variance in density is exactly what it is all about. We usually work from one end of the wall to the other – there is little need to fear joins as careful sensitive work precludes such. Refrain from oversponging, but should this occur you

can always sponge over a dense spot or a smudge using the base colour – and no one will ever know. Remember to wash the sponge every now and then to prevent clogging. You should have a bucket of water handy to pop it into when the phone rings. A second layer of sponging in the same or a paler tone will break up the texture even more to produce a better finish.

The corners and recesses could prove to be a problem since one either oversponges, cannot reach or smudges. A quartered sponge with flat planes and sharp angles could help,

but it is much safer to leave corners undersponged than to overwork them. Oil-based sponging needs to dry overnight before you sponge over it and sponges must be cleaned with turpentine, brush-cleaner and water.

The texture provided by a natural sponge is ideal for the recreation of granite. If you use a white background and sponge a light sprinkling of pure black all over, and follow that with a number of grey tints getting progressively paler with each sponging, a lovely black-grey granite emerges. Other possibilities are black and sea green or grey and brick red.

Dragging

WATER-BASED DRAGGING

A decorator called us in one morning to paint a guest cloakroom for some overseas clients. A little problem was the fact that the painting was promised for that afternoon! She requested a dragged surface below dado level, a softly rubbed wall above and a sympathetic leafy stencil in between. Thanks to the quick-drying properties of Polvin and Glazecoat, the clients were delighted when they arrived to a finished job in the afternoon.

A base of Polvin or Double Velvet is ideal to work on. The colour is to your choice but, unlike in the case of sponging, we prefer to drag a darker tone onto a paler base. Mix a water-based glaze with one part Polvin (PVA –

in any colour) and one part Glazecoat. Since you use very little glaze it would be inadvisable to mix large quantities. A small quantity of glycerine will help to deter drying.

Load a brush with some of this glaze and drag it onto the surface. Select a brush with a texture to give you the brushmarks you prefer: fine, medium or coarse. Aim to establish the required brushmarks as soon as possible, moving from top to bottom, even painting right into the recesses and corners. This process is called dragging-on – once the glaze is painted on, you have little time to move it before it dries. Once dry, it is irrevocably settled. This sounds daunting but once you have the knack, you can complete an entire quest cloakroom and bathroom in a morning.

OIL-BASED DRAGGING

The slow-drying oil glazes allow you to fidget and fiddle for much longer. But given this, you still need to realise the physical limitations of oil. Would you be able to drag a very high wall running up and down a ladder? Base coats for all oil glazes must be Satin Sheen Enamel (Plascon Velvaglo). These must be quite dry before you can work on them. An oil-based glaze made up of equal parts of Velvaglo (usually a darker colour than the base), Scumble Glaze and mineral turpentine should be used. Also mix a quantity of film former as follows: one part of mineral turpentine, two parts raw linseed oil and the tip of a teaspoon of Terebine Driers.

Rub the film former onto the surface area before it is glazed. Just a thin film of this oily mixture allows the glaze to be manipulated over that surface. The glaze is painted on as a thin translucent coating stretching all the way from the top to the bottom. Use a dragging brush to drag the area in straight lines from top to bottom, removing excess glaze and revealing the base colour. This is called dragging-off. Push or stab the ends of the bristles into the corners at the top and the bottom before you drag the middle stretch. Slightly wavy or slanted lines are not a problem, but a straight batten used as a ruler could aid your straight-line endeavour. Drag over and over until you feel satisfied or until the glaze goes "off" or becomes too thin. Leave a narrow band of glaze – a wet edge – in which to start the next part.

Finding a dragging brush – which has rather long pliable bristles – can be problematic, but rest assured that any brush that provides the linear effect you want, can be used. You can even take an old brush, snip out some bristles here and there with a pair of scissors and use it to create a rough, rustic, dragged texture.

Once you become familiar with dragging, you can use it as a base for woodgraining. A beige background dragged with white could evoke the appearance of limed beech, while a yellow-cream background with dark oak varnish dragged across it could be mistaken for oak.

A dragged surface executed in silken colours could be softly dragged horizontally just before it dries. Thus the impression of slubbed silk can be created and used to great advantage in a classical French interior: walls lined with silk!

Rag-rolling

The third of the evergreen trio is quite as simple as its name implies. We grew up with grey Formica kitchen cupboards, tables and chairs – contrasted with primary reds, yellows and blues – all textured to resemble perfectly regular rag-rolling. The one thing we avoid doing is to demonstrate rag-rolling in any of those 1960s colours because someone is bound to shout "Formica!" But the real thing can be infinitely more beautiful and again there are various colours, intensities, contrasts and textures within the parameters of this technique. Having read the section on dragging-on and dragging-off (page 125-126) you will understand ragging-on and ragging-off as well.

WATER-BASED RAG-ROLLING

Until a slow-drying water-based glaze is produced in South Africa all water-based rag-rolling will have to be "rolling-on". The glaze mixture should be old hat by now: one part Glazecoat, one part Polvin (PVA). Prepare a wall with a background colour of your choice. Crumple a sizeable piece of lint-free rag into a sausage shape but do not screw it into a tight form. Roll this rag through a shallow puddle of glaze in a paint tray or an enamel plate. Roll it lightly over a sheet of blank newspaper to remove any excess glaze. Also check the impression which your cloth will make. Proceed to roll the rag across the wall following a roughly diagonal direction. Work systematically, covering the wall with ragged imprints. Rearrange the cloth from time to time in order not to produce the same pattern in endless repeat. Obvious repeats, like a big fold in the cloth, must also be changed for the same reason. Once a cloth has become too sodden it must be discarded for a new one. As in sponging you can roll the base colour over any unwanted blotches to make them disappear. Moving into corners where the rolling motion cannot reach, you need only to dab the cloth gently. Try not to smudge or spill onto adjoining areas. A smaller cloth would perhaps be the answer.

OIL-BASED RAG-ROLLING

Velvaglo Satin Sheen Enamel will be the best base for this technique. Any colour will do if you bear in mind that the glaze that goes onto it should either be darker or deeper in tone.

You need no specialist tools: some mutton cloth, some lint-free cotton or similar fabric, a regular paintbrush (50 mm or 75 mm), some film former and some basic glaze (see *Oil-based dragging* on page 126). Use a piece of mutton cloth to rub a modest amount of film former onto the area to be rag-rolled initially. Bear in mind that this must be no more than a thin film of oil. Prepare an odd shape rather than a perfect square or rectangle. Paint a thin coat of glaze over the area. The brushmarks must be eliminated and the easiest way to do it would be to roll a piece of mutton cloth into a loose pad and to use it to smoothen out glaze. A soft patting/pushing movement following a figure of eight works well. Another option is to use a stippler brush or jamb duster to stipple the entire surface to attain uniformity. At last the rag can start rolling. Crumple and twist the cotton rag into a cylindrical shape. Roll this little sausage across your glaze, preferably on a diagonal. Leave a wet, unworked edge where the work will be continued. Rub film former onto the next part, glaze it and work right into the wet edge.

Follow the dabbing and rag-rolling procedure again. You can certainly do with an extra pair of hands and if a friend will work in tandem with you, rag-rolling is quick and easy. Remember that neatly ragged corners, a relatively even hand and neatly wiped edges are a sign of superior work.

Finishing coats are not essential on any of these techniques but if extra protection is required, the water-based surface can be finished with two or more coats of Glazecoat Gloss (REF. 1124) or Matt (REF. 1125). Oil-based surfaces can be varnished. Woodcoat Polyurethane Varnish Suede Coating is our preference and at least two coats are required. If the Suede (Matt) is still too shiny you can apply three coats, allowing for perfect drying in between. Continue by rubbing the whole surface down gently with very fine waterpaper. Do not be distressed if your beautiful handiwork turns dull white! An application of a good wax polish brings the colour out again and once it is buffed up, a lovely soft patina manifests itself.

Polyurethane coatings may in due course turn yellow which in the case of blue or white painted objects can be disastrous. If this is a problem an oil-based Glazecoat (Plascon CV82) is available to provide a durable finish. It is quite glossy though. But follow the instructions above to turn the gloss into a sheen!

The red conservatory

White bagged walls were not exactly the right home for this well-used potting table, old oil painting and terracotta pots. Fascinated by the turn-of-the-century warehouses and their red brick walls, we decided to use shades of red to enhance these walls. Various coats of glazes produced an extraordinary depth and brilliance. A terracotta-tiled floor, old terracotta pots, patinated baskets and an "antique" painting provide accessories to a soulful interior.

The red conservatory: Step by step

1. Initially the entire wall, which was painted in White Polvin (PVA), was rubbed with a glaze mixture of one part Jumbunna Orange Polvin (T69-5 Plascon Computacolor) to two parts Water-based Glazecoat Matt (REF. 1125). An ordinary bath sponge was used. Already at this stage one can pick out irregular patches of bricks to be given a more generous coating of glaze. By now the general appearance is very anaemic and uninspiring.

2. Repeat the whole process, sometimes applying more dark glaze onto some brick patches as well as creating a few more patches. Take care, from the outset, to work glaze neatly into all the nooks and crannies, being fastidious with the finishing line at the cornice.

3. The third coat of glaze consists of one part Tennent Creek Orange in Polvin (PVA) (T69-7 Computacolor) mixed into one part Plascon Water-based Glazecoat Matt (REF. 1125). Rubbed on as were the previous coats, but without picking out bricks, it provides a deeper tone as a film over the entire wall, toning down the picked-out bricks. The brighter red glows through beautifully from underneath but can be darkened in the corners, or in selected areas to create contrast and interest. The end result provides a room filled with atmosphere, ideal for lazy sunny afternoons. No finishing coat is needed as the Glazecoat component provides the tenacity.

Accessories

The table was acquired from a restorer who was poised to restore this rather rickety but characterful piece. Cleaned up, it found its way into the conservatory lending a "tatty-chic" look! Old plant pots, straw, blackened old baskets and other conservatory or potting shed items continue the theme. The painting on the wall in its simple black frame is a reproduction, painted recently in the naive style by a Frenchman living in Egypt. Flanking it are two curly metal brackets, most probably a 1960s left-over, still with their very own black paint and rust, planted with trailing ivy.

Terracotta floor tiles combine happily with the ruddy walls and provide a visually pleasing and practical surface for such an area.

A look conceived

We cannot remember any more how our relationship with Constantia Uitsig began. Somehow we were called in to paint their breakfast room. Driving up the avenue of bluegum trees for the first time, we could already feel the serenity of this corner of the Constantia Valley. While there were builders, landscapers and farm folk at work everywhere, everything seemed to progress to a steady rhythm rather than rushing and gushing towards no particular end.

*O*nly our most gentle and sophisticated sample boards were considered, and under the discerning gaze of the owner we created a series of temperate finishes.

The restaurant was born later and the really interesting work started. With a rapport having been established, we were briefed on the type of restaurant, the furnishings, colour preferences and the extent of painting needed. A decorator friend of the owner displayed the most remarkable feeling for both her friend's preferences and the Constantia ambience. The rural quality was a very important ingredient and could under no circumstances be disregarded. Searching for actual colour references we walked through the overgrown garden and came upon an old weathered fountain with an ochre patina, patchily invaded by green moss … we had found the colours with which to start!

The initial painting was in the newly added conservatory from where one can gaze out over the vineyards to the mountains etched against the blue sky. The French distressed walls were the result of two rubbings with a colour from the International Colour Chart (Gold Pheasant 8-18D). A heavy cement table

was treated with the same colour and, imitating the lovely old fountain, rubbed with some green (International Colour Chart Sea Green 55-9U). Eventually a most relaxed picture emerged, marrying French, English and Cape looks.

Subsequently more and more painting was done – always using the Gold Pheasant range of colours as a departure point. Thus the bar area became heavily distressed with rich browns and reds complementing the rich wooden fixtures. A lounge was treated in three soft rubbings to create a soft but nonetheless effective background for English florals, cerise and calico. In time the fireplace has smoked a bit, leaving a homely dusting of soot up the mantelpiece.

Even the garden was not forgotten: two large cement pots painted in red stoep paint now reside in tatty "old fountain" splendour at the bases of the Norfolk pines. What a splendid place in which to work or laze, watching the seasons come and go, the greening of the oaks and vineyards, the ripening of the wheat and the weathering of the garden walls – colours which were invited indoors.

Media

Our aim with decorative painting is to apply colour to surfaces of plaster, wood, metal, etc., using various media. These media are usually made up of two or more components, the most important of which are pigments and vehicles. Knowing the properties of the vehicles allows you to apply solvents or thinning agents where and when they are needed.

An understanding of these three elementary components can facilitate your work immensely.

Pigments

Colour is a natural phenomenon. Natural pigments or colours are so much part of our lives that we hardly notice them: the red of beetroot, the black of soot, the yellow of clay, the rich red-brown of tea. Whereas the Egyptians had to grind their own pigments and the pioneers had to discover their own stains we, today, have the advantage of obtaining our pigments ready-made. Many are still natural but a wide spectrum (and a range of qualities!) of synthetic pigments have been developed.

Pure powdered pigment is available and ranges from bags of yellow ochre, red and black oxide by Polycell and so-called "school powder paints" or tempera powders right through to very refined artist's pigments available only from specialist artist's supplies dealers. Pigments in liquid form are often referred to as universal stainers and are used extensively in the world of decorative painting.

Vehicles

The vehicle or liquid part of paints or glazes carries the pigments and other ingredients (such as resin, binders, solvents or driers). All of these are then held together once they have been spread across the surface.

Solvents

The formulas of pigments and vehicles sometimes need to be diluted, moved, wiped away or cleaned up. Solvents are used to these ends.

The simplest solvent we know is water and we use this with wet acrylic (PVA) paints or, even more basically, with powder or "school" paints. Most of us also know how to clean brushes with turpentine or paint thinners, while the solvent properties of methylated spirits cannot be underestimated. However, these cannot be used at random. Every vehicle requires its own solvent. It is imperative either to read the labels on paint or glaze tins carefully or to seek advice before using a solvent impulsively. Water does not clean off oil paint!

Care must be taken: good ventilation is required with most paint work. Be particularly careful when using thinners; do not have any open flames around and refrain from smoking.

Develop an awareness concerning your media – get to know their properties so that you can play with them. Sensitive people may react to some solvents and it is only prudent to take care of your health by wearing protective gloves and masks.

Glazes

Now, understanding the basic composition of paints and glazes, we can be more specific. Some reference to history might help us to understand the nature and use of glazes in decorative painting.

Nowadays we are used to paints that have maximum coverage, leave no brushmarks and have admirable qualities developed by modern science. Throughout history man had to produce his own pigments ranging from crushed rock to vegetable juices and blood. The vehicles used also varied – from egg yolk to milk, fat and oil. It follows that painters had to have a very sound knowledge of their media. Even so we discover old painted surfaces with the striations of brushmarks, undulating colour, interesting crackling, chipping and flaking.

To obtain these picturesque and fascinating finishes today we need to adjust modern paints to render them "imperfect", and create glazes. The nature of these mixtures provides us with media that are translucent and opaque and that will retain impressions. The glaze must be liquid enough to manipulate easily, but it must not run down vertical surfaces. On the other hand, it must have some body without being pasty. A varnish with some pigment added would, for instance, provide a coloured (opaque) translucent finish, but no opportunity to create interesting imprints because it dries too rapidly.

We hasten to add that varnishes should not be referred to as glazes – it will not only cause confusion when interpreting instructions, but especially when purchasing products.

The Dutch masters used to work with oil glazes. Starting with brilliant flat colour on the canvas they superimposed various translucent coloured glazes, layer upon layer, building up depth of colour, form and dimension. Every school formulated their own glazes and stories abound of secret recipes being passed on from master to apprentice.

OIL GLAZES
Various recipes are available and they can range from simply equal quantities of boiled linseed oil and turpentine (called megilp) to elaborate combinations including oil, turpentine, beeswax, carriage varnish, driers and even some whiting. A superb ready-mixed oil glaze – Plascon Scumble Glaze – can be purchased off the shelf, eliminating all experimentation and the heartaches of depressing failures.

WATER GLAZES
A distinction should be made between washes and glazes. Where water is used as a medium or where water-based paints or PVA paints are diluted and thus used to impart a thin film of colour, it is known as a wash.

A glaze has more substance and carries the pigment. Only a few years ago we had to contend with patent mixtures like water, beer and pigment; water, vinegar, sugar or fuller's earth and pigment. In fact, these still provide a special quality which we insist on using for certain effects. Once again a modern product is available to use as a base for a water glaze – Plascon Glazecoat, Gloss or Matt. This product has many subsidiary uses but you need time to get used to these.

Tools

*H*ardware stores fascinate us! The older they are, the better. Tall shelves full of neatly arranged tins, carousels with a variety of brushes, bins with sponges, rolls of sandpaper, rolls of plastic sheeting, rolls of mutton cloth … how does one decide!

Collecting the proper tools for the trade could cost hundreds of rands or almost nothing. Appropriate tools include essentials such as rags, mutton cloth, sponges, paper, feathers, etc. Some effects need specialist brushes and rollers but these can be acquired bit by bit. Initially expensive and sophisticated equipment can quite easily be substituted with inexpensive tools. You may even discover suitable equipment that is better than the regular tools.

Brushes

Art and hardware shops stock a great variety of brushes. They vary in size, shape, bristle and, obviously, purpose. The following is a short list of brushes available locally:

- Regular 20 mm, 50 mm, and 75 mm flat paintbrushes.
- An array of artist's hoghair brushes, flat and round.
- A jamb duster or hoghair softener, 75 mm. Used for stippling small areas or for dragging.
- A dragging brush. The long bristles form excellent striations.
- A block stippler, 75 mm x 100 mm. Used for stippling larger areas.
- A flogger – for woodgraining or dragging.
- Badger-hair softeners, 40 mm and 75 mm – for softening of marbling.
- A hak brush. This is a very soft, Japanese watercolour brush and can replace a badger-hair softener.
- Stencil brushes of various diameters.

General tools

- Natural sea sponges. Acquire various sizes and textures; each one is unique.
- Synthetic bath sponges. You will find the coarsely textured specimens at any super-market.
- Graining combs, rubber.
- Enamelled tin plates, cream or any other plain colour.
- Enamelled tin mugs.
- Measuring cups (medicinal measures will do).
- Plastic or old metal spoons.
- Feathers for marbling or graining.
- Scissors.
- Artist's knives, NT cutters or Stanley knives – with extra blades to keep in stock!
- Rollers and trays – both the water-based paint rollers and the smaller ones for oil-based work.
- Plastic buckets – various sizes.
- Mutton cloth – for general wiping and cleaning.
- Laundered rags – a variety of textures and weaves would be handy, to be used for rag-rolling.
- Sandpaper – different grades, especially some 80-grit.
- Protective gloves.
- Generous aprons or overalls.
- Plastic sheeting or other drop sheets.
- Masking tape of various widths.
- Mallet for closing tins of paint.

Taking care of your tools

An aspect which can be very trying is keeping your workshop and tools neat and tidy. The joy of finishing a project is often marred by the thought of cleaning up. Once you get into a routine it becomes easier, though.

CLEANING OFF WATER-BASED MEDIA

If tools have been used in water-based media like emulsion paints, they must be cleaned immediately after use. Wash them thoroughly under running cold water. If you are interrupted while painting or sponging, rather stand the brush in or drop the sponge into water until you can resume work. Squeeze brushes and sponges to remove as much water as possible. Brushes should dry hanging or lying down. If they are stood up in jars or tins, the metal parts (ferrules) fill up with water and paint which, when it dries there, will render the brushes hard and useless.

CLEANING OFF OIL-BASED MEDIA

Because oil takes longer to dry you have more time at your disposal, but leaving oily tools overnight is taking it too far! Oil paints or glazes on tools must be dissolved in turpentine or Polycell Polyclens: wiggle the brush in paintbrush cleaner and squeeze it out. Rinse under cold water. Repeat the process if there is still too much paint on the brush. Proceed to immerse only the end of the brush in some Polyclens paintbrush cleaner and work the cleaner well into the bristles. Rinse under running cold water. Use plastic gloves when working with brush cleaner and work in adequate ventilation. Try not to get the cleaner into the ferrule as it will loosen the bristles, and do not use it on plastic material.

Try to avoid the use of brush cleaner on badger-hair softeners and hak brushes. Rather use turpentine to dissolve and rinse off the glaze, then use ample detergent (dishwashing liquid) and cold water. It may sound peculiar but our badgers are frequently subjected to a shampoo-and-conditioner treatment; after all, what is good for us must be good for a badger! Bear in mind that these brushes need protection against moths if they are to be stored for any length of time.

South African equivalents of overseas products

It is the rule rather than the exception that decorative painters start off with the absolute basics, virtually no tools of the trade and paint straight from the tin. Reading English or American publications often adds to the confusion when one is confronted by unfamiliar terms and names. It is hoped that the following list will help to put things into a South African perspective!

SOUTH AFRICAN TERMS	FOREIGN TERMS	SOUTH AFRICAN TERMS	FOREIGN TERMS
Designer's colour	Gouache	Scumble glaze	Glaze medium
Dragging	Strié	Solvent	Thinner
Film former	Megilp	Steel wool	Wire wool
Key	Tooth	Sword liner	Dagger, sword striper
Knotting	Shellac, knot sealer, button polish	Terebine driers	Siccative, driers
		Turpentine	Paint thinner, white spirits
Lining brush	Script liner brush		
Matt	Flat, matte	Universal stainers	Tinting colours, colourizers
Methylated spirits	Denatured alcohol	Universal undercoat	Primer, standard undercoat
Mutton cloth	Stockinette		
Pure turpentine	Mineral spirits	Varnishing	Finish coats, varnishing coats
PVA emulsion paints	Latex paints, emulsion paints	Velvaglo Satin Sheen Enamel	Alkyd, flat oil
Sandpaper	Glasspaper	White Wood Glue	PVA

Index